Is Graduate School Really for You?

IS GRADUATE SCHOOL REALLY FOR YOU?

The Whos, Whats, Hows, and Whys
of Pursuing a Master's or Ph.D.

....

AMANDA I. SELIGMAN

The Johns Hopkins University Press
Baltimore

© 2012 The Johns Hopkins University Press
All rights reserved. Published 2012
Printed in the United States of America on acid-free paper
9 8 7 6 5 4 3 2 1

The Johns Hopkins University Press
2715 North Charles Street
Baltimore, Maryland 21218-4363
www.press.jhu.edu

Library of Congress Cataloging-in-Publication Data

Seligman, Amanda I.
    Is graduate school really for you? : the whos, whats, hows, and whys of pursuing a master's or Ph.D. / Amanda I. Seligman.
        p.   cm.
    Includes bibliographical references and index.
    ISBN-13: 978-1-4214-0460-8 (hardcover : alk. paper)
    ISBN-13: 978-1-4214-0461-5 (pbk. : alk. paper)
    ISBN-13: 978-1-4214-0482-0 (electronic)
    ISBN-10: 1-4214-0460-5 (hardcover : alk. paper)
    ISBN-10: 1-4214-0461-3 (pbk. : alk. paper)
    ISBN-10: 1-4214-0482-6 (electronic)
        1. Universities and colleges—Graduate work—Handbooks, manuals, etc. 2. Graduate students—Handbooks, manuals, etc. 3. Dissertations, Academic—Handbooks, manuals, etc. I. Title.
    LB2371.S56 2012
    378.1'55—dc23   2011021672

A catalog record for this book is available from the British Library.

Special discounts are available for bulk purchases of this book. For more information, please contact Special Sales at 410-516-6936 or specialsales@press.jhu.edu.

The Johns Hopkins University Press uses environmentally friendly book materials, including recycled text paper that is composed of at least 30 percent post-consumer waste, whenever possible.

To my friends from graduate school, especially Jared, Graham, and Rebecca, who did so much to get me through; and with special gratitude to Ricki, who inspired this book

Contents

....

5. Dissertations and Theses 64

6. The Academic Culture 82

7. Having a Life in Graduate School   102

8. Degrees, Jobs, and Academic Careers   116

Afterword   134

Preface

....

Every year in the United States, hundreds of thousands of students who aspire to earn master's degrees and doctorates start graduate school.[1] Many new graduate students know a lot about their fields of study, perhaps having pursued them as undergraduate majors or worked as research assistants on professors' projects. Others are discipline changers or autodidacts, who explored their topics individually, outside of standard education tracks. Some have obtained advanced degrees in their native countries but are new to the U.S. system of education. However much new graduate students know about their fields, most know little about graduate school. Unless they were raised in a family of academics, enjoyed excellent undergraduate mentoring, or pursued a graduate degree previously, the experience of graduate school itself is probably new, unfamiliar, daunting, and exhilarating, all at the same time.

The purpose of this book is to demystify the institution of graduate education in the United States for people who do not yet know much about it. I describe how people decide where to earn a master's or doctoral degree, financial issues, academic culture, the processes of graduate education, and job prospects. The main focus is how graduate school works. I also include "voices," comments from real graduate students reflecting on their experiences. "Expert Tips" from faculty and other experienced students provide guidance on some of the stickier situations graduate students find themselves in. The sources for these quotations are provided in a separate section at the end, preceding the endnote references. A glossary at the back of the book defines academic terms that may be unfamiliar. Finally, a bibliography suggests further reading, especially for people seeking detailed advice about succeeding in graduate education.

This book is written for people who want to know more about what graduate school is like, whether they are thinking about applying to programs, are already enrolled, or just want to understand what education beyond the college level entails. Undergraduates can learn about how to apply to the programs of their choice and what to expect there. Current graduate students can use it as a roadmap through their programs. International students may find that the U.S. system's expectations differ from their home-country norms. People who love graduate students but do not understand how they are spending their time will find straightforward explanations of the process. This book focuses primarily on the liberal arts rather than the kinds of professional training offered by M.B.A., J.D., M.D., and other degree programs.

One of the things biggest hurdles in graduate school is the thesis or dissertation, a project that is usually essential to completion of the degree. It is hard because producing original scholarship for the first time is more than just coming up with new ideas; it also entails engaging in an unfamiliar process of research and writing. A student must figure out how to manage a large-scale, independent scholarly project at the same time as understanding a phenomenon no one has ever explained before. The same thing is true of graduate school at large. Graduate school, in the liberal arts, at least, is not just an extension of the undergraduate degree. As one of my friends explained in the orientation to my doctoral program, the point of the exercise is to change the student from a consumer of scholarship into a producer of scholarship. Figuring out how to navigate this transformation—an intensely personal one—makes graduate school scary and exciting at the same time.

The information and advice I offer come from a range of sources. I first imagined this book when I was studying for my doctorate in American history at Northwestern University and teaching ethnography alongside sociologists and anthropologists. They taught me that I should understand what I was *doing* as well as what I was *studying.* When I took a position as an assistant professor at the University of Wisconsin–Milwaukee, my advisor suggested that I write down all the things that confused me about the institution so that when new colleagues came along, I could ease their way by sharing these tidbits. So while I studied as a graduate student, had friends who were graduate students, and taught graduate students, I also played ethnographer, paying critical attention to the ups and downs of their experiences, the things that they needed to learn about academic life, and what they understood intuitively that I had to learn the hard way. As I researched this book, I conducted written surveys of graduate students to discover what they thought should be included.[2] I also read regularly in such online discussions as the forums of the *Chronicle of Higher Education* online and *PhinisheD.org*. To round out the gaps in my knowledge, I read advice manuals, scholarship, and other reflections on graduate education. Quotations from these accounts are displayed in these pages as "Voices" and "Expert Tips."

Although I offer advice about navigating the strange institutional cultures that graduate students encounter, I make no pretense of telling readers how to succeed in graduate school. Beyond the shared and implicit goal of graduating, not all graduate students have the same purpose in mind when they enroll. Some students enroll in master's programs in order to learn about something they got only a taste of in college; others see their degree programs as a way of learning new skills that will increase their value in the private sector. Many doctoral students know that earning a Ph.D. is a prerequisite to winning a job as a professor, but not all their peers share that aspiration. Significantly, many students' goals change over the course of their studies. Some decide that, after all, they do want to be professors; others realize they hate academic life and want nothing more than to drop out of their programs with their dignity intact. Because of the variety of their ambitions, I believe that no single model of success can guide all students through the process. Instead, each graduate student needs to understand how his goals articulate with the culture of his field of study.

I strive in these pages for a neutral description of the culture, expectations, and experiences of graduate school. Other scholars have written books with more direct advice about how to succeed in graduate school. Such books, whose merits vary widely, are listed and described in the "For Further Reading" section. Many assume that every graduate student starts at 22 years old, wants to be a professor, will not consider any other career, and is willing to put his or her personal life on hold for the time it takes to earn a graduate degree (and probably tenure as well). My hope is that by describing what graduate study is and how it works, readers will be able to work out for themselves what they need to do to satisfy their particular purposes.

Although I aim for evenhandedness in my descriptions of graduate school, it is inevitable that someone who has spent her entire adult life in the university setting will have strong opinions about graduate education. I was a graduate student for seven years, have taught graduate students at the University of Wisconsin–Milwaukee for more than twelve years, and have directed a graduate program for the past four. My opinions are embedded into this book as assumptions about what is important to include and exclude, and it seems only fair to explicate them here.

1   Going to graduate school is a crucial life choice. It opens up many new personal and professional paths. Graduate students are not postponing "life" by starting graduate school; rather they are *having* a life. Other normal aspects of life that need tending—family, personal relationships, health, spiritual well-being—do not disappear simply because a student has taken this particular path.

2   Because graduate students are having a life, they must not neglect their own health. Graduate students ought to attend to their physical and mental health by eating right, getting sufficient exercise, and enjoying (a moderate amount of) relaxation time. Graduate students who become physically ill or experience a mental health crisis like clinical depression

should take care of their medical needs, not single-mindedly forge ahead with work.

3   Graduate school is not only for 22-year-olds fresh out of college. Even in the sciences and mathematics, which are reputed to be a young man's game, it is possible for students to begin graduate study well after completing an undergraduate degree. In the humanities and social sciences, years spent in other arenas prepare a graduate student in both work discipline and observational skills crucial to developing the kinds of trenchant analysis that the academy values above all else.

4   In most academic fields, there is only one way to get a job as a professor: earn a doctorate first. So graduate school is full of aspiring professors. However, not everyone who goes to graduate school starts out or ends up wanting to be a professor. A host of other important and respectable motivations impel students to devote years to graduate study.

5   As a corollary, if a prospective position is not right for him, a graduate student who has successfully earned his doctorate does not owe it to his advisor or the department that trained him to take a job as a professor. Choosing a nonacademic career is legitimate. Graduate programs that value their students as people and not just as protégés will include training in alternate career paths as part of their program of activities.

6   Graduate school can have a transformative effect on students. When my mother began to study for the ministry, she learned that "if seminary doesn't change you, it's not working." Graduate school similarly has the capacity to change how students see and act in the world, at the level of changing their values. That is normal, and a sign that the student is paying attention.

7   Graduate school is optional. Unwise though it perhaps is for someone with a vested interest in the continuation of graduate study to point this out, graduate school is not essential to anyone's life. Graduate school should be a pleasure, fun,

interesting, and worth a student's time. When graduate school becomes just a grind and not a reward in itself, it is time to quit.

How to Use This Book

This book is written in a question and answer format. You can read the book from start to finish, choose the chapters that interest you at any given moment, or hone in on the question you are most interested in—the questions are listed in the table of contents. If you are thinking about applying to graduate school, you might want to start with chapter 1, which discusses the decision to go to graduate school and the application processes. If you have been admitted to graduate school already, you might find chapter 2, on financial matters, most pressing. If you are working on your thesis or dissertation, you might skip ahead to chapter 5, which addresses the research process. If you are the parent of a graduate student trying to make sense of the decision your child has made about how to spend several valuable years, chapter 3, on graduate expectations, or chapter 6, on academic culture, might be most useful to you. However you use this book, I hope that it helps in understanding that graduate school entails navigating both a fascinating field of study and a complicated institutional culture. The book will help you to understand what graduate school is like. Put that together with what you know about yourself and you should come away knowing if graduate school is right for you.

Acknowledgments

Every current and former graduate student that I ever met has in some sense helped me think about the contents of this book. I would like to offer special thanks to the following people, who shared their ideas, provided me feedback on the manuscript, and provided technical assistance: the students who filled out my survey; the anonymous peer reviewer; Ellen Amster; Anita Cathey; Nelida Cortes; Sean Forner; James Michael Hill; Mandi Isaacs Jackson; Margaret King; Nick Landau; Bonnie Lynn-Sherow; Kerry Mueller; Michele Radi; Martin Seligman; and Merry Wiesner-Hanks. Karen W. Moore provided research assistance for which I am most thankful. At the Johns Hopkins University Press, I am grateful to Ashleigh McKown for believing in the value of this project; to Greg Nicholl and Deborah Bors for shepherding it through production; and to Dennis Marshall for copyediting the manuscript.

I would also like to express my gratitude to the members of my immediate family: Joe, Sophonisba, and Irene. Although they mostly stop me from doing as much work as I think I should, they remind me every day how to be an academic and have a life at the same time.

Is Graduate School Really for You?

CHAPTER 1

So You Want to Go to Graduate School

....

It seems like a miracle that I have survived academic life for twenty years. When I applied to graduate school, I made so many naïve mistakes that it is a wonder that I was accepted into any doctoral program. Despite having grown up in an academic family, I failed to seek advice on a whole host of matters, including what programs I should apply to. I was changing fields from classics to history and probably should have pursued an M.A. before seeking admission to a doctoral program. I thought I wanted to be a professor one day, but mostly I just wanted to know more about history. Before I left my undergraduate campus, I did not ask my instructors in history classes for letters of recommendation, which made tracking them down and reminding them of my existence a real burden (this was before e-mail accounts were widespread). I did not research the faculty of the programs I was applying to; nor did I read any of their scholarship. I did somehow know enough to send in a writing sample from a class I had taken in my new field instead of my old field. In retrospect, I can see why most of the programs I applied to rejected me. I was just lucky to get into a great program and find the perfect advisor. Fortunately, I was a quick study, and from that shaky foundation I learned my way around my new discipline and academic life. But my story could have turned out quite differently.

This chapter provides an overview of what prospective graduate students need to consider about their individual situations and about how the admissions process works. There is little about graduate education that is universal, but it is always the department and faculty, not the larger university, that decide whom to admit. As a consequence, there is no single guide to the minimum standards that indicate a student can get into graduate school, while even the most qualified on paper may not be admitted to her choice of programs. Researching a potential program can pay great dividends in ascertaining a fit between an applicant and the people who decide who gets in.

What motivates people to pursue graduate study?

Earning a professional graduate degree such as an M.D. is a perfectly rational choice for prospective doctors: the degree is a prerequisite to having a career as a physician, and most people who earn M.D.s attain jobs in the field. But a graduate degree in the liberal arts does not offer such a straightforward deal. On one level, pursuing a master's degree and then a Ph.D. makes the same kind of sense for someone who aspires to be a college professor: it is increasingly difficult, almost unheard of, to be hired as a full-time, permanent member of a college or university faculty without a Ph.D. In the twenty-first century, even community colleges can take their pick of highly qualified candidates and they routinely hire Ph.D.s for their tenure-track positions. Because an earned doctorate does not guarantee winning a job, the benefits of going to graduate school are less obvious.

Nonetheless, there are some pragmatic and career-advancing reasons for going to graduate school. Some professions, such as teaching, industrial research, and curating museum exhibits, require postbachelor's degree credits, value the content and skills acquired by students with advanced degrees, or offer greater pay to people with master's and Ph.D. degrees. Going to graduate school in an academic discipline can also sharpen the analytic skills that will be employed in later professional studies such as law or business.

Sometimes graduating seniors decide to go to graduate school because they have not found work in their chosen professional field. It is a commonplace observation that graduate school applications rise in bad economic times and fall when entry-level jobs are plentiful and well-paying. By riding out a recession in graduate school, students prepare themselves to be productive members of society while exploring a field of potential interest.

The best and most idealistic reason for going to graduate school is to learn in a relatively systematic fashion about a discipline one simply wants to know more about. In many subject areas it is possible to read on one's own during leisure time, but to deeply understand what is going on in a field, the guidance of professionals who read and produce such scholarship is indispensable. In addition, having an abiding passion for a field is the best way of getting through graduate school with a minimum of angst and a maximum of satisfaction. For many people who find graduate school's material rewards to be few, the intrinsic pleasure of learning new things and producing new knowledge keeps them working—and working eagerly—from day to day.

Should a student go to graduate school immediately after finishing the bachelor's degree or wait a few years?

The answer varies with the discipline. In some disciplines, it does not matter much; entering cohorts of graduate students include a healthy mix of students fresh out of college and nontraditional students. The conventional wisdom in the hard sciences and especially mathematics is that students must enroll in graduate school shortly after finishing their undergraduate degrees because the most brilliant work is done by people under thirty. In fields like sociology, anthropology, and history, where people are the object of study, a few—or many—years spent out in the "Real World" can aid the student's insight into the human condition, so waiting to enroll can be a real benefit to the student's scholarship.

Students who decide to go to graduate school several years after finishing their undergraduate degrees face a couple of difficulties, none of which is insurmountable. The first, practical hurdle comes in the application, which requires obtaining letters of recommendation from professors familiar with a student's work and able to assess their potential for success at the graduate level. As undergraduate professors' memories of a student's work fade, it becomes harder for an applicant to obtain a useful letter of recommendation. The undergraduate who is planning on going to graduate school in a few years should ask her current professors to draft a letter immediately, to be sent out when the time comes.

Additionally, students who spend years employed or raising children before attending graduate school may find that that they do not have the same energy, available time, or intellectual intensity as their peers still in their twenties. This apparent gap may feed the normal insecurities about their fitness for the work that most graduate students feel. They may resent subordinating themselves to faculty members who are younger than they are. But maturity and experience can help older graduate students handle the other

> **VOICE:**
> Many of the just-out-of-undergrad students in my cohort found grad school very hard, for various reasons: not accustomed to scheduling own time, not accustomed to managing so many details & deadlines without being reminded constantly, not accustomed to working, going to school, and not having a social life, etc. I often had to endure 15 minutes of whining at the beginning of certain classes . . . often to the point that the professors had to say, pretty clearly, "Stop whining and do the work."
>
> —Prephd, re "Why is grad school so hard?"

standard psychological hurdles of graduate school with more equanimity than their younger peers do.

Is a master's degree a necessary prerequisite for getting a Ph.D. or a job as a professor?

Not usually. Some graduate programs do require applicants to have a master's degree or equivalent credits for admission, but many do not. Some programs routinely and without ceremony award their doctoral students master's degrees after they have completed a specified number of credits. Search committees probably never notice whether the Ph.D.s they hire have master's degrees, since possession of a doctoral degree implies ability to do master's level work in the same field.

I can offer a personal example: I do not have an M.A., although I earned one. I enrolled directly in a Ph.D. program that required few prerequisites, and when I became eligible for the M.A. I did not have the $50 graduation fee required by the university. If I had left graduate school before completing the doctorate, however, I would have applied to graduate with an M.A. so that I had something to show for my time. The availability of an M.A. as a "consolation prize" for students leaving doctoral programs is widespread.

Is it possible for a student to go to graduate school in a discipline other than one studied as an undergraduate?

Yes. Some graduate programs have prerequisites that specify the number of credit hours within the field or in particular skill sets that applicants must demonstrate. But other programs take promising students whose records do not suggest existing competence within that field. Sometimes it is possible to take graduate courses at a local public university without being formally admitted to a program in order to show admissions committees that one is serious and capable of working in the field. This strategy also can help an aspirant gather letters of recommendation from faculty familiar with her potential to work in the field.

How are admissions decisions made?

At undergraduate institutions, it is typical for a dedicated admissions staff to make decisions about whom to admit, whom to waitlist, and whom to reject, no matter what field students intend to study. At the graduate level, however, such decisions are left to the faculty of the student's program. The rationale for this practice is fourfold: (1) graduate programs usually receive fewer applications than the undergraduate college, so it does not make sense to employ people solely to evaluate admissions; (2) expertise within a field is necessary to assess an applicant's potential for success; (3) taking on a graduate student as an advisee is an important, long-term commitment, so faculty need the opportunity to decide whether they want a given person to work under their supervision; and (4) in programs that fund their students through teaching and research assistantships, an offer of admission is usually an offer of employment as well, and only expert faculty are qualified to judge employability in a specialized lab or classroom.

The faculty in different programs delegate admissions decisions in different ways. In some programs at the master's level, the decision is made solely by a director of graduate studies. In other programs a faculty committee reviews applicant files and decides collectively, by majority vote, a competitive bidding process, or consensus. Especially at the Ph.D. level, the admissions committee may also circulate an application to potential advisors and ask whether they are willing to "take on" a given student.

Students in the sciences may have to be accepted into a lab where they will conduct research as well as into the general graduate program. Once the pool is narrowed to admissible candidates, the faculty may argue with one another about whom actually to let into a small program, allowing a particular professor to recruit a dream student in exchange for a promise to reject all applicants who want to work with that person in the next admission cycle. This kind of horse trading, which is understandably kept invisible to students, helps explain why an applicant should not take rejection from one or a few programs as a general comment on her abilities.

How many applicants do graduate programs accept?

The selection criteria of graduate programs vary widely. Most programs use the same basic set of application materials, with only minor variations: a statement of purpose, Graduate Record Exam (GRE) scores, transcripts of prior education, letters of recommendation from professors, and sometimes writing samples. But admissions committees that decide who gets in and who gets funded treat those materials differently.

Programs with the greatest prestige generally receive and reject the most applications. A high-ranking program may have space for only a few dozen new students each year but receive several hundred applications. When admissions committees want to recruit the cream of the crop, they often are looking for excuses to set aside quickly most applications. In an effort to narrow the field to a manageable number for serious scrutiny, these admissions committees may simply dismiss out of hand files from students whose GRE scores or grades are below the norm for the pool or some predetermined cutoff point. Some programs expect applicants to state which faculty member they want to study with, effectively creating a secondary application pool that only one or two students may swim in. Even a talented student may be a poor match for the particular focus of a program and find his application treated accordingly.

Obscure, student-starved, and low-ranked programs admit much higher percentages of their applicants, who typically number fewer than those of better-known programs. But even less-sought-after programs usually reject students who do not appear prepared for advanced study in their field. Faculty members who decide on student admissions do not want to waste their own time—nor the energy of students who will not do well.

Rejection from a given graduate program does not necessarily mean that a student cannot succeed in that field in the long run. It might simply mean that the applicant was not among the most competitive who applied in that year. It might mean that the admissions committee could not see how the student's research interests meshed with the existing faculty or the university's resources or that institutional politics prevented their admission. Consistent rejection from multiple graduate programs, however, might suggest that the student should revisit his plans for graduate study. One strategy for dealing with rejection is to show the application materials to a trusted faculty member and ask for a candid assessment of future admissions chances and guidance about what next steps to take.

An additional consideration is whether the admitting institution has minimum qualifications for graduate students, such as having attained a certain undergraduate grade point average. A program may prefer to admit a student whom the university would automatically reject; in some cases, it may be possible for a student to enroll on a probationary basis with strict criteria for retention, such as maintaining a B+ average in the program.

Should a prospective graduate student pick a school or a program?

The particular program that a student enrolls in matters much more than the school itself. A student may be tempted to attend the university with the most famous undergraduate education, but this inclination is not always wise. Although rich schools can pay faculty well and buy the most comprehensive libraries and cutting-edge equipment, they do not invest equally in all graduate programs. The prestige of a graduate degree (within the academy, anyway) derives from the reputation of the program, which is a function of the perceived quality of its departmental faculty, not of general institutional fame and wealth.

That said, it does matter where a student attends graduate school, especially if he aspires to work as a professor. While a Ph.D. is a Ph.D. no matter who granted it, who supervised the dissertation remains important. Well-networked supervisors can help their students get a foot in the door for jobs, fellowships, and other research opportunities. Faculty search committees do consider the reputation of the advisor and degree program when they look at applicant CVs.

The program itself also matters to the graduate student's own life experience. A disorganized or otherwise unfriendly home department can make a graduate student's life miserable, while a program that recruits a congenial group of fellow students and laboratory staff can set the stage for happy years in school. Students who are picking degree programs do well to consider both the reputation of the program within their discipline and the general esprit de corps of the established graduate student body.

Are online graduate programs respectable?

Academic administrators across the United States believe that the future of higher education lies in putting degree programs online. The list of institutions offering undergraduate courses and even entire degree programs online has multiplied many times since the start of the new century. For many bricks-and-mortar colleges and universities, putting courses online seems like a surefire way of increasing revenues: without having to spend extraordinary new sums on space or faculty, they can enroll more students. For institutions that exist primarily in cyberspace, expansion from undergraduate programs to graduate degrees is a classic no-brainer. Although there are many fewer graduate programs available, their numbers are increasing. The respectability of online programs varies with discipline, so prospective online students should consult with people in their field about programs they are considering.

Students who are contemplating enrollment in online graduate programs should carefully consider their postdegree goals. A student whose desire for graduate study is purely avocational might benefit from an online degree program as much as a traditional program. A student who wants to use his degree as a credential for advancing his career should conduct informational interviews with likely employers ahead of time to find out what their views of the program are. In any case, before applying to an online-only degree program, a prospective student should research whether the institution is fully accredited and in good standing in its home state or is a diploma mill that trades money for credit, with no return of learning. Questions to ask the program representative include the accessibility of library materials, availability of faculty via e-mail, and how learning that traditionally has required face-to-face contact—such as labs and practica—will be covered.

What equipment does a graduate student need?

When I completed my undergraduate degree in 1991, my grandmother offered to buy me a typewriter as a graduation present, not realizing that I had owned a computer since the time I was a freshman. Specific disciplines have specialized equipment demands, but it is hard to get by these days without a computer. A laptop is particularly useful for graduate students who need to travel to do research, while certain software packages are essential in some fields. Highly specialized equipment needed for scientific research is paid for out of grants or built on the spot, not financed out of a student's pocket. The best way to find out what personal equipment a new student needs is to ask a current graduate student or professor.

Graduate students also need a place to do their work, pile up their papers, and store their research materials. This might mean a quiet space in an apartment or a separate office. One of my friends in graduate school rented a studio apartment that he used exclusively for work. In some universities and departments, graduate students are provided with office space as routinely as faculty members are.

Students who are members of grant-funded project teams are usually provided with working space. At most institutions, however, space remains at a premium even in this age of online education and the only graduate students afforded workspaces are those employed as research or teaching assistants.

How do graduate students finance their education?

The "college fund" is an American staple, but undergraduate education is so expensive that few families set aside money to pay for a child's graduate education. Yet graduate school, which can take much more time than a four-year undergraduate degree, is very expensive. A hidden cost of graduate school is foregone earnings: while their peers with bachelor's degrees hop merrily off to the world of paid jobs and discretionary income, graduate students sacrifice years of salary in order to pay for yet more education. Fortunately, the options for paying for graduate school are quite extensive. In addition to the standard array of possibilities (holding down an outside job, receiving financial aid, parental support, and taking out loans from banks and the federal government) graduate students may be enticed into choosing a particular school by the offer of a stipend from the university, either just for enrolling or in exchange for doing some form of work.

The standard advice for Ph.D. students is not to attend a program that does not pay his or her way through a combination of fellowships, grants, and teaching and research assistantships. The next chapter examines the financial issues graduate students face.

CHAPTER 2

Financing Your Education

....

One of my colleagues was the first in his family to be a full-time graduate student. The family expected anyone who had been fortunate enough to graduate from college to be self-supporting—to make good money and to brag about it. At family gatherings, when they asked him about his earnings, he was embarrassed. From the perspective of a graduate student he was doing fine: his tuition and health insurance were covered by the university and he received a monthly stipend that paid for a room and shared kitchen in a local apartment in his expensive city. But to make himself sound more successful, he added together the value of his stipend, his tuition, and health insurance, and he told them that that substantially heftier figure was what he was earning. In one sense, he was correct—he was *earning* that much money, even if he saw little of it in his checking account. But then he could not explain why he was living so modestly and accumulating credit card debt.

Graduate school does not provide the kinds of immediate financial rewards that an idealist might wish. Some students pay out of pocket or take out loans to attend, while others live on small stipends provided by fellowships and assistantships and moonlight to make ends meet. In either case, the amount of time graduate students put into their studies represents time in which they could have been earning money at much higher rates than they receive from their universities. On the plus side, universities do allow graduate students to keep body and soul together in a variety of ways that prepare them for their future careers as researchers and teachers. This chapter outlines the variety of financial opportunities that make graduate school manageable though not lucrative.

What forms of financial aid are available to graduate students?

Students in graduate programs are usually eligible for a variety of forms of financial aid. Master's students are only rarely offered the kinds of assistantships described in this chapter and have to find a way to support themselves and pay high tuition bills at the same time. Ph.D. students, however, should be wary of financing their education with loans. Thanks to grants brought in by faculty, funding for doctoral studies is almost universal in the sciences; it is available but less frequent in the social sciences and humanities.

The standard advice for doctoral students who plan on becoming professors is not to enroll in a Ph.D. program unless someone else —preferably their university or a prestigious national fellowship— is financing their education and underwriting their basic living expenses. In many disciplines, especially in the humanities, fewer than one-half of the people who complete their doctorates get jobs as professors, so accumulating personal debt with this goal in mind is usually not prudent. Most doctoral programs have some money, doled out in the form of assistantships or fellowships, to entice the most promising applicants to enroll. Students who are admitted but not granted this kind of institutional financial aid generally are regarded as high-risk or medium-quality students; that is, the institution feels it cannot justify investment in them because they probably will not do the kinds of research or get jobs that advance scholarship significantly and enhance the doctoral program's reputation. Some doctoral programs do not finance any first-year students, preferring to reserve financial assistance as an incentive for students who have proved themselves worthy by surviving a first-year weeding process.

Graduate programs typically have some combination of two

broad classes of financial assistance available to select students: assistantships and grants. To receive assistantships, students generally have to work at something other than their own studies. The most common forms of assistantships are research assistantships and teaching assistantships. Assistantships require a large time commitment, but they also serve as professional training that prepares graduate students for future roles as faculty members with teaching and research responsibilities. Grants and fellowships typically do not require any work beyond that required for the degree, but this does not mean that they come without strings attached. Many assistantships are meant to cover the academic year only, leaving students without funding in summer, when school is not in session.

Students who hold research assistantships (RAs) are usually expected to work for a professor in some capacity that draws on and develops their own capacity for scholarly work. The research may range from doing an odd list of tasks that the supervising professor has whimsically thought up on the spot—or so it seems to the student—to conducting formal and mostly independent experiments in the laboratory. In the sciences, RAs join a lab funded by a professor's grant and are expected to conduct research that supports the lab's larger projects. RAs in labs may be told what experiments to conduct or they may get to design their own projects within the parameters of the professor's scholarly agenda. Some RAs are given few, if any, formal responsibilities and so find themselves with the equivalent of a fellowship for a semester or two. Other RAs, however, are assigned grunt work such as returning library books or photocopying for faculty members too swamped to do their own mundane tasks.

Teaching assistants (TAs) either run small group sections of a larger lecture course or actually teach their own courses. When working on a larger course, TAs typically meet with their supervisors and other TAs to discuss the trajectory of the class, run quasi-independent discussion, problem, or laboratory sections, hold office hours, field e-mail queries from students, and grade undergraduate exams and homework. TAs running their own classes may work from a departmentally mandated syllabus and textbook or might design the course from scratch, autonomously. Some departments hire their own graduate students as adjunct instructors, without TA status. Depending on the financial arrangements of the university and whether graduate student assistants are unionized, an appointment as an adjunct instructor might pay better—or worse—than being a TA. Students in the sciences who are primarily supported as RAs can round out their CVs and prepare themselves to be professors by working as a TA for a few semesters.

Fellowships and grants encourage students to focus all of their energies on their formal studies and their own research, from coursework to dissertation. These forms of assistance are offered by universities, the federal government, and national foundations that support particular fields of endeavor. Fellowships (and scholarships) tend to be awarded on the basis of an applicant's general excellence and fit to the criteria of the fellowship. A fellowship stipend may support a student for as little as a semester or as long as several years. Grants, on the other hand, tend to support particular projects or pieces of a project, such as a trip to a distant library or field site.

The fact that grants and fellowships support the student's own research does not mean that they are easy money. Application processes are generally competitive and labor-intensive. Winners may find themselves with unexpected obligations and opportunities, like traveling to meetings with other fellows or the sponsors or giving public talks on their work. Recipients of grants may be expected to commit to work in a certain region after graduation in exchange for accepting the award. Winners who do not complete their degrees may be pressured to refund the investment in their unfinished research.

> **EXPERT TIP:**
> TAing can take a lot of time away from other things so, although it looks good on a résumé and carries some weight when one is being considered for a faculty position, *you do not want to do it more than a few times, if possible.*
>
> —Bloom, Karp, and Cohen, *The Ph.D. Process*

Both assistantships and fellowships may carry conditions that affect a student's educational program or future plans. Many, for example, require recipients to maintain a particular grade point average. Some require students to be enrolled for a certain number of credits, which might result in a student taking classes that she was not particularly interested in or did not need in order to graduate. Because applying for such awards can be time-consuming, it pays to study the requirements before completing the paperwork.

Why do universities pay graduate students to attend?

Undergraduates are not paid to earn their degrees. Even student-athletes are technically prohibited by NCAA rules from receiving gifts and salaries in exchange for their services. Universities expect to receive high tuition dollars from students in professional degree programs, such as those earning M.D.s, J.D.s, and M.B.A.s. But students in the liberal arts are routinely (and rightly) advised not to enroll in any graduate program where the university is not paying their way. It may seem like a paradox: American society rewards holders of practical professional degrees with high salaries but underwrites the educations of people who hope to become low-paid (if high-status) professors.

There are two major reasons that universities pay tuition, health insurance, and stipends to the bulk of their graduate students. First, universities pay graduate students to enroll because it is their mission to advance research, much of which graduate students produce. Graduate students on fellowships often receive a stipend for doing nothing more than thinking, researching, and writing. Universities are in the business of producing new knowledge. That is why they allot faculty members time for scholarship as well as teaching.

Extending funds to the most-talented graduate students accomplishes the same goal. When graduate students produce strong theses, dissertations, and articles, the glory reflects back on their home institution, enhancing its reputation as a contributor of new ideas to society.

But universities also get relatively cheap labor from graduate students. Postdoctoral students and graduate students are the people who conduct the bulk of scientific lab research because faculty members' time is consumed by teaching, conceptualizing projects, writing grants, and supervising the production of publications. Reliance on graduate students as teaching assistants has become common, to the extent that some universities now depend on TAs to provide much of the face-to-face instruction provided for undergraduates. Many universities simply could not educate their large undergraduate student bodies without graduate students to run discussion and lab sections, to grade the reams of exams, and to assist faculty research. For substantially less than the cost of a faculty member's salary, universities can hire smart, motivated, and interesting people to interact with the student body. If professional degree programs had undergraduate counterparts, universities might consider hiring medical and law students to teach undergraduates, too.

What size stipends do universities offer graduate students?

Graduate stipends are typically not large or generous. A student who is qualified to go to graduate school would almost always do better financially by taking some other job. Students who live on their graduate stipends usually calculate that they are trading several years of genteel poverty for a professional life they can attain in no other way. Universities generally set their assistantship rates to provide for a student's basic needs for shelter and food, but little else. Certainly, they do not expect the funding to be sufficient to support either personal luxury or a family. In 2006, a food bank in Calgary, Alberta, noticed that graduate students were among its regular clientele.[1] Some universities post their standard assistantship rates on their Web pages, but at other institutions these rates vary by department.

Although the stipends themselves are low, they typically come with an array of benefits that increase the value to the recipient. The biggest, most significant benefit of graduate stipends tends to be free tuition for the length of the assistantship or fellowship or at least a waiver of out-of-state rates at public universities. Students may also receive, depending on which institution they attend, health insurance or treatment at a campus clinic, free or reduced-cost access to university events, child care that is subsidized or on campus, and gym privileges.

VOICE:

To keep their labs up and running, scientists need funds (commonly hundreds of thousands of dollars per year) to pay for supplies, equipment, animals, and salaries of graduate students and postdocs (and even portions of their own salaries). Funding is their most basic concern.

—Bloom, Karp, and Cohen, *The Ph.D. Process*

Where does the money for graduate assistant stipends come from?

Although from the perspective of a graduate assistant stipends provide relatively paltry funds, for universities the costs of providing for the education of graduate students add up significantly. Since university administrators recognize that it is impossible to run a reputable and competitive graduate program without incentives to lure the best graduate students to enroll, some graduate student funding is built into base budgets. Then there is external funding. Scientists keep up a continuous search for such funding through grant applications. Although equipment costs certainly factor in, a significant portion of most research-grant proposals is salary and tuition for graduate assistants. Nonscientists, too, are increasingly encouraged to bring extramural funding into the university to pay a variety of costs, including those of graduate research assistants.

What is adjunct teaching?

Many American colleges and universities supplement the teaching of their full-time, tenure-track and tenured faculty with people who are hired to teach on a semester-by-semester basis. Adjunct instructors go by different titles at different institutions; frequent terms include ad hoc, contingent, and temporary faculty. Adjuncts may be fully credentialed, published Ph.D.s, holders of terminal master's degrees, or students working toward their doctorates. Sometimes adjuncts teach just one course, one time; at other times, adjuncts teach the equivalent of a full-time course load for many years, effectively making a career of temporary contracts. Typically, adjunct instructors receive low pay and lower status (they even may be denied office space in which to meet their students) and have little control over the scheduling of their courses. Generally, institutions hire people as adjuncts for two reasons: (1) to offer their students courses that their regular faculty are not taking on; and (2) because they can.

Why do highly educated professionals accept the working conditions of adjunct faculty?

Even though adjunct teaching brings few material or social rewards, many graduate students and people with completed degrees accept such positions. Their reasons are myriad. Some have moved on to other careers but enjoy having student contact. Many recently graduated adjunct instructors seek to build up teaching experience on their CVs so that they will be attractive candidates for more stable positions. Some continue teaching as adjuncts for many years while they seek a tenure-track position that they will never achieve. Others have cobbled together sufficient work at different institutions to earn a living that they find comfortable, a practice that is particularly possible for people whose partners have jobs that provide health insurance and more reliable salaries.

Why do some graduate students join unions?

Graduate students often have two distinct relationships with their universities: their studies make them students, but their financial packages also make them employees. Many graduate students work as researchers and research assistants, instructors and teaching assistants, and administrators and assistants for their universities. Insofar as graduate students think of themselves as employees, some are inclined to protect their rights collectively and call for improved working conditions, wages, benefits, and hours. The American court system, however, is split as to whether or not graduate student employees are eligible to organize unions. In some institutions, especially public universities, graduate student unions are long-established and uncontroversial. At other universities, administrators have fought fiercely to keep their graduate students from organizing legal unions, arguing that they are students primarily and workers only incidentally.

If a graduate student can work as a teaching assistant or even an adjunct instructor, is completing the degree still worthwhile?

The fact that graduate students can find work teaching in their fields even before their degrees are completed would seem to suggest that a Ph.D. is not, in fact, a prerequisite to making a living in college teaching. It is, however, increasingly difficult to have a career as a college-level instructor without the completed credentials.

It is well-nigh impossible (not to mention intellectually unsatisfactory) to make a career out of being a teaching assistant. The major reason that being a TA for life is an untenable strategy is that appointment as a TA is usually contingent on student status and offered only for a limited number of years. Even if a department tried to hang on to a long-time teaching assistant, many universities impose time-to-degree limits on their students to encourage them to complete their degrees in a timely fashion. In addition, departments typically also decide to award TAships to graduate students who are advanced, but not too advanced, also as a way of encouraging them to finish their theses. The withdrawal of financial support is supposed to be an incentive to graduate. Students in the humanities and social sciences who reach the maximum number of years offered by their departments to serve as TAs often turn to adjuncting to support themselves.

Many graduate students do manage to live for years on the relatively paltry wages of adjunct instructors, but teaching on a course-by-course contract can make for a vicious cycle. In order to make enough to support themselves, especially in expensive cities, adjunct instructors must take on multiple courses, which can stretch out research and writing times and thus make finishing the dissertation even more expensive. Some adjunct instructors work for many years without completing their terminal degrees.

But completion of the Ph.D. provides the keys to the kingdom—or, at least, the opportunity to grab for the keys to the kingdom. A position as a permanent faculty member, either tenured or on the way to tenure, is what provides job security, salary, health insurance, opportunities for advancement, and status in the profession. It is getting rarer for colleges at any level to hire tenure-line faculty members without the Ph.D., simply because so many people with doctorates apply for those jobs. Even community colleges, which have typically valued commitment to teaching over research experience, hire mostly Ph.D.s. So while it is possible to step off the degree-completion track and still teach college, doing so leaves the adjunct instructor stranded at the bottom of the professional hierarchy.

Should a graduate student take a job outside the academy while completing a dissertation?

Most institutions fund their graduate students through fellowships and teaching and research assistantships for a finite number of years. A standard, though sometimes unrealistic, expectation is that students complete their degrees in five years. At some point a graduate student who works slowly but is determined to finish must figure out how to support himself independently while he completes the degree. Many graduate students faced with this question turn to adjunct teaching. Other graduate students find administrative jobs at their home institutions as a way of staying connected to their academic community. Still other graduate students, decide to take a "real world" job while they plug away at the dissertation.

There are advantages and disadvantages to taking a job outside the academy. Not only is the employed graduate student faced with the normal dilemmas and choices that beset workers who are not also students, she must give some consideration to how her planned job fits with her future career. For a graduate student who does not intend to stay within academic life, getting a job that helps her build a résumé and relevant professional experience is a great idea. A future professor must think about the demands of a nonacademic job and their effect on her dissertation and teaching prospects. A low-stress, routine job can provide enough money and emotional space to work on a dissertation. A demanding job with higher pay can crowd out the "leisure time" and energy that should have been reserved for research and writing, but it might also serve as a starting point for a fulfilling, nonacademic career. But a nonacademic job does not fit neatly on an academic CV, so the student must consider how to explain that gap in time and academic experience to a faculty search committee.

Should a graduate student accept a job as a professor before graduating?

Because graduate students are so poorly paid compared with their peers and because the academic job market is so crowded, many future professors begin their job searches as soon as they can plausibly make the case that their dissertations are near completion. For some graduate students, this means applying for jobs as soon as they are All But Dissertation (ABD, meaning they have completed all the requirements for the degree except the dissertation). Most strike out until their dissertations are finished, but a lucky few receive offers to join the tenure track. If the dissertation can be defended before the student leaves for the new position, there is little danger. But a continuing student who starts working as a tenure-track professor runs the risk of never completing the degree. A new faculty member may be surprised by the difficulty of balancing the development of multiple new courses, the demands of professional service, and the culture shock of a new hometown and watchful senior colleagues with the need to reserve several hours a day to work on the dissertation. It may be easier to deal with the day-to-day deadlines than to chip away at the research, writing, and revisions needed to satisfy the dissertation committee back at the student's graduate institution.

Graduate students who are members of underrepresented minority groups should be especially wary when the lure of the tenure track is dangled before their eyes. Although minorities are still subject to a variety of forms of discrimination, the American diversity culture means that colleges and universities are anxious to advertise high numbers of nonwhite faculty members. With too few graduate students of color in the pipeline, there are simply not enough to burnish the reputations of all the institutions that would like to develop a critical mass of minority faculty. The resulting fierce competition for underrepresented minority faculty means that some graduate students are tempted into tenure track positions too early and at institutions well below their true capabilities. One of my friends from graduate school had the perspicacity to recognize the worth of his scholarship and carefully held himself off the job market until his dissertation was everything he wanted it to be. Only then did he allow employers to court him. One of the last of us to graduate, he was the first of us to achieve the rank of full professor—and it was in the Ivy League.

CHAPTER 3

Graduate Expectations

Shortly after Thanksgiving during my second year in graduate school, my grandmother died unexpectedly. I do not remember packing to go East or how I got there. I do vividly recall, however, sitting at my grandparents' dining room table surrounded by an enormous stack of library books I needed for my final paper in my African history course. I must have dragged those books with me from the Midwest. After the memorial service, the rest of my family dispersed back to their normal lives, but because my graduate student instincts had kicked in when I was packing, I found that I already had everything I needed to finish out the quarter. So I stayed on with my grandfather for several extra days while I worked on my paper and we both worked on our grief.

Graduate students enjoy enormous amounts of flexibility and autonomy in determining the pace and locale for their work—but their work does not go away just because life intervenes. I knew that if I did not get that paper done by the time the new quarter started, I could have an incomplete hanging over my head for a very long time. Graduate students' choices about how to balance work and life may seem inexplicable to outsiders, but they are often driven by the relentless character of academic work, especially for people who are just starting out. This chapter reviews some of the unwritten rules that shape how graduate students decide when and how to chip away at their enormous workloads.

Is graduate school more demanding than college?

Yes. Graduate school is harder than college. It is not simply an extension of college or the undergraduate major—graduate school is a different enterprise altogether. Going to graduate school is like joining a major league baseball team after years in the summer softball league. Undergraduate majors are expected to learn content and to understand how basic research in their discipline is produced. Graduate students, however, are trained to conduct and write about the field's research on their own, a different task with very different demands.

A student who received mostly As as an undergraduate may be quite surprised to discover he is not an A student in graduate school. Most of the people motivated enough to attend graduate school did fairly well in college, but the grades graduate students receive differentiate among a much narrower pool of competition than that undergraduates face. A similar quantum leap of talent levels can also manifest as a student moves from a master's program to a Ph.D.

How is graduate school different from professional education in medicine, law, and business?

The fundamental difference is that professional schools seek to inculcate in their students specific knowledge that will enable them to function in particular work contexts. Graduate school, by contrast, aims to teach its students how to produce new knowledge and ideas in their fields.

> **VOICE:**
> Graduate students learn not only how to teach undergraduates but also how to produce some of what undergrads study.
>
> —Clark and Palettella, *The Real Guide to Grad School*

Important differences flow from that basic distinction. Professional schools with a prescribed course of study take a specified amount of time to complete, while graduation from an M.A. or Ph.D. program depends on completing certain hurdles, especially

VOICE:

All [professional schools] involve professional skills that depend on studying different objects—electrical as opposed to chemical engineering, the physiology of the skeleton as opposed to anesthesiology, the law applied to shipping as opposed to entertainment. Moreover, medical schools and law schools, unlike the humanities and social sciences, train people to practice their professions outside academia and have a licensing system.

—Clark and Palettella, *The Real Guide to Grad School*

the thesis, that take an indeterminate amount of time. Therefore while professional schools have distinct entering and graduating classes, graduate students are unlikely to graduate with the same cohort of people they started with.

Finally, almost everyone pays to study in professional school, either out of their own pocket, with family support, or through loans. Graduate schools, however, often pay their students a modest stipend and tuition in exchange for work as a teaching or research assistant or as a reward just for participating.

How is going to graduate school different from a full-time job?

It certainly benefits graduate students to treat their work in a professional manner. Students who go about their work in a disciplined fashion, set aside regular hours for studying, and treat their professors and classmates with appropriate courtesy will probably end up with healthier selves, relationships, and careers.

There is, however, at least one significant difference between graduate study and a "real world" job. An employee tends to have a boss who, in theory at least, sets her priorities and establishes deadlines. By contrast, the work required in graduate school tends to be structureless. While still taking courses, students have to show up for classes and turn in assignments at relatively regular intervals, but they decide when and where to do the work—at the library, in the coffee shop, in bed, or not at all (with the only consequences for the last being failure). This formlessness manifests itself acutely at the thesis stage, when the student is certified to go forth and pursue a major research project, from beginning to end, on his own. Although students have advisors, those advisors are not their bosses. Students decide when to spend time on research (including when and for how long to travel, if needed for the project), when to spend time writing, when to spend time just thinking, and when to goof off. For some students, this freedom is exactly what they wanted, especially after rigid time demands of previous jobs. For others, this structurelessness is terrifying and paralyzing, slowing down their progress toward the degree. One consequence of working on one's own timetable is that graduate programs often lack the sense of social cohesion that cohort membership in a college or professional degree program provides.

In some disciplines, the tendency toward structurelessness is at least partially ameliorated by the demands of research. Scientists who run experiments have to show up at perhaps inconvenient but predetermined times to adjust the lab equipment. Astronomers wait to take scheduled turns at the telescopes. High-energy particle physicists reserve slots at the accelerators to run their experiments. Students conducting archival research are stuck working within the hours set by the library. Botanists and archaeologists must go into

---

VOICE:

I don't really find grad school any more challenging intellectually than I did undergrad (but I thought my undergrad institution was pretty challenging). I think what makes grad school hard for many people is not so much the work itself, but the amount of it, and the fact that once you finish course work, you pretty much have to self-schedule your time. No one really hold[s] you to deadlines anymore, and it's up [to] you to figure out how much time to put into things. That can make it feel like you should put ALL your time into your work, and obviously causes people to burn out.

—Krolik, re "Why is grad school so hard?"

---

the field in the right season to observe their grasshoppers or dig up their shards. The push of institutional factors such as these can help distractable students discipline themselves. Especially in the sciences, where advisors double as lab supervisors, research assistants may be expected to show up on predetermined schedules, with vacation and sick leave established by contract.

How many hours per week should a graduate student expect to spend working?

The amount of time required to succeed in graduate school varies with the demands of the particular program, the nature of the discipline, and the student herself. The amount of time required to do the coursework phase of graduate programs differs according to subject. Some courses, such as those in philosophy, require lots of reading that can be completed only slowly, with close attention to the significance of each word. Other disciplines reveal differences in student aptitude; they may assign problem sets that can be done quickly by those who grasp them right away but only slowly by most students. Reading lists for key exams can range from a few preselected critical works of scholarship to a dizzying, general charge, such as "go and master this field of literature."

The amount of time required to do original research for a dissertation also varies according to discipline. A graduate student in anthropology may have to spend a year "in the field," possibly abroad, constantly observing the culture in which he is immersed. A historian who needs access to archives may be able to use them only during business hours. This can be frustrating for someone who is willing and able to spend 80 hours a week poring over old documents, only to find that the archive is open for only 40 hours a week. A student in biology may be able to accomplish little of apparent use during the intervals while her experiment "cooks," but have to show up in the laboratory and attend to the petri dishes during odd moments in the middle of the night or on weekends. In *Getting What You Came For*, Robert Peters describes his own travails in simply obtaining the fish he planned to study: "It took me two years to figure out how to breed enough of them for experiments. Unfortunately, you don't get extra points on your Ph.D. for figuring out that swordtails kill each other in close quarters."[1]

Finally, the amount of time devoted to study depends in part on the student's own situation. A graduate student with small children might be able to work only while her children are in daycare, adding some apparent drag time to her program; but if she is efficient she might actually accomplish twice as much as her peers in a given amount of time. A student with strong eyes might be able to spend many more hours peering at microfilm than a student who has to

---

VOICE:

- 6:30–8:00 AM: Drink coffee, make breakfast for the kids while they prepare their lunches, get everyone fed and dressed, and get kids to school and preschool.
- 8:00 AM–noon: Attend or teach classes, exercise for 1 hour 3 days/week, volunteer at the preschool or in Jacqueline's classroom 1 hour/week, work part-time job 10 hours/week, research or attempt to write a fabulous dissertation.
- Noon–3:00 PM: Pick up Paul from half-day preschool and enjoy time with him, often joined by my mother; run errands and do chores as "fun time."
- 3:00–8:00 PM: Drink coffee, pick up Jacqueline from school and enjoy time with her and Paul until kids' bedtime.
- 8:00 PM–1:00 AM: Drink coffee, research on line, and write.

—Angelica Duran, "One *Mamá's* Dispensible Myths and Indispensible Machines"

VOICE:

A doctoral student in mathematics once explained to me why math graduate students appear to have so much leisure time available for non-work pursuits. Math, she said, is so hard and requires so much concentration that it is just impossible to devote more than a few hours a day to research before one's head explodes. So after spending her allotted several hours on research, she went out and enjoyed herself ice skating.

---

take a coffee break every couple of hours. Some graduate students prefer to treat their studies as jobs that start at 9:00 AM and end at 5:00 PM, as is the case in some professional pursuits; others are willing and able to throw themselves body and soul into the work for a few years. Part of the task of graduate study is for the individual to figure out what research patterns are most productive.

What characteristics are most valuable for success in graduate school?

Surprisingly, brilliance is not the most important personal trait needed in graduate school. Of course, students do need a certain facility for their fields. A person who is bad at math simply will not be able to understand advanced physics. Similarly, someone who is monolingual cannot hope to receive a degree in comparative literature. But these are matters of basic smarts, not of outstanding intellect. Instead, people who make it through graduate school are most likely to be possessed of high levels of intellectual curiosity and stamina.

Graduate students simply must be interested in their work. Graduate school takes too long, requires too much undirected work, provides only ambiguous status, and offers too few material rewards to sustain the attention of someone who does not find her studies intrinsically satisfying. Graduate students need not only to understand the materials that professors present to them but they must also have enough curiosity to pursue their own questions without guidance. A graduate student who is bored with his classes, his readings, and his research will not be motivated to finish the degree.

> **VOICE:**
> What is the most important ingredient for success in graduate school? Many might answer "brilliance." I, however, would choose "resiliency."
>
> —Steven M. Cahn, *From Student to Scholar*

> **VOICE:**
> A dissertation is not a "paper." I can't just go to the library for a few hours, pull an all-nighter, and be done with it.
>
> —infopri, re "Wish your family understood"

> **EXPERT TIP:**
> If you find yourself lacking the energy to read a George Eliot novel on your own, leave graduate school now.
>
> —Gregory M. Colón Semenza, *Graduate Study for the Twenty-First Century*

In addition, graduate students need to be able to run an intellectual marathon. Writing a thesis or dissertation usually takes at least a year, if not more, of relatively undirected labor. In contrast to an undergraduate term paper, even a poor dissertation cannot be thrown together at the last minute. Without a commitment to researching and writing at regular intervals over a long stretch of time, a graduate student will not be able to complete the central, capstone project.

Finally, having a high tolerance for being alone helps. Graduate students have to spend a lot of time by themselves, reading, thinking, and writing. This can be hard on extroverted students, who are likely to find graduate school isolating. One charming graduate student I know does all his work in coffee shops, but he has to change his spot every couple of months because he automatically turns his workplace into a social gathering. Such students may do brilliantly in their coursework—a situation thick with other people—and then founder at the dissertation stage, which may require much more time spent alone.

How does learning occur in graduate school?

Graduate students do most of the learning on their own, essentially self-directed. Because the goal of the process is to create an independent researcher, someone who can produce new knowledge and ideas, it makes sense that much of the process is solitary.

Students also glean a significant amount of learning from their classmates and postdoctoral students through casual, unstructured conversation. Other students are often at the cutting edge of a research field and can explain what is interesting and what is not, and why. As Bloom, Karp, and Cohen explain in *The Ph.D. Process*, "It is understood in academia that those who know have some obligation to teach those who do not, and spontaneous, on-the-spot instruction on 'this' or 'that' is common."[2] This informal education from peers is a very quick and relatively easy way to figure out a field's intellectual landscape.

Finally, students learn from professors, both in the classroom and, sometimes, outside. But professors rarely top the list of who taught a given graduate student the most important lessons. Especially in the sciences, professors are often too busy with the work required to generate funds to be in the lab themselves, keeping up with the latest techniques. The graduate students and postdocs who execute the research projects are more likely to know *how* to do the work, while the PI keeps her eyes on the *whys* and the significance of the research. Professors may tell a student what to read or how to modify their research method, but only rarely do they deliver content directly, orally, to the students' ears.

> **VOICE:**
> While solitude may stimulate creativity, scholars do not flourish in isolation. They depend on publishers, librarians, research associates, and most important, one another.
>
> —Steven M. Cahn, *From Student to Scholar*

What do graduate students learn?

Part of what graduate students learn is content and technical skills specific to their fields. Historians learn about what happened in the past; physicists learn about how the universe works; language specialists read literature in their language of study. But most of what graduate students learn about is process: how to do research, what is known or unknowable in their fields, which tools are good for making which kinds of discoveries, how to make an effective argument, how to teach their discipline, how to think like their professors, and how to manage their workload. In order to figure out what the unanswered questions are, graduate students have to understand how their fields work.

Graduate students can also learn about academic culture—the topic of this book. If they pay attention to the right opportunities, they can learn about how to get through their programs, the mistakes to avoid, about academic politics, how to prepare for the job market, what academics reward, how to get published, and many

---

VOICE:

What makes graduate school "so hard" is that it is a total commitment (not quite 24/7, but it feels like it) and it lasts in that near-24/7 mode for a *long, long* time. Many people don't have the energy, time, and interest, along with the intellectual curiosity and rigor, necessary to go through all that. When they try, they find it overwhelming. Even people who have what it takes find it overwhelming at times.

—Infopri, re "Why is grad school so hard?"

VOICE:

There are lots of brilliant people who don't make very good academics. Some of them never made it into academia, and others slide on through, with a not very successful academic career. On the other hand, there are lots of successful academics who aren't all that bright (dare I say that? I guess I do), but who have done very good work in teaching, in research, or in both.

—John Goldsmith in *The Chicago Guide to Your Academic Career*

---

more topics. While not everyone pays attention to these matters, every graduate program offers an introduction to the academy and disciplinary norms, not just to the field itself.

Do graduate programs expect all of their enrolled students to graduate eventually?

Some programs hope to keep as many of their students as possible. They make financial and emotional investments in people they believe are most likely to succeed, and the faculty regret seeing anyone depart. Other programs anticipate high attrition rates in the first few years. Some programs are even structured to winnow out a certain percentage of each incoming class through a series of difficult exams or other forms of intellectual hazing. Students tend to learn through the grapevine which kind of program they are enrolled in. It is possible to research this question during the application process by talking to current students.

What are the attrition rates in graduate programs?

The number of students leaving without a degree varies, depending on the program. Doctoral students in engineering, science, and mathematics are more likely to complete their degrees than those in humanities and social sciences.[3] All advanced degree programs experience some attrition because predicting student success is difficult. While it is often possible to tell from applications who is most intellectually capable of doing the required work, projecting whose temperament will enable the student to take a graduate degree to a successful conclusion is an inexact science. And, because graduate school is entirely optional, some students are bound to drop out along the way. Bowen and Rudenstine write that, in contrast to professional schools, where about 90 percent of students graduate, "only about *half* of all entering students in many Ph.D. programs eventually obtain doctorates (frequently after pursuing degrees for anywhere from six to twelve years)."[4] Bowen and Rudenstine worry that this high attrition rate is bad for the academy and reflects poor decision making in admissions. But many personal factors, including a rational look at the job market, also help explain why some graduate students choose not to complete their degrees.

Why do some graduate students drop out of their programs?

It is rarely an easy decision or a bad idea for a student to leave his or her graduate program. Most of the rewards of graduate school are intrinsic. In contrast to other professions that require advanced degrees, an academic degree does not necessarily translate into extrinsic rewards such as high pay, status, or even a guaranteed job. If a student feels unhappy or dissatisfied as a graduate student, the chances are good that he or she will feel equally discontent as a professor, which is, after all, the major line of work that doctoral degrees formally prepare people for.

People drop out of graduate school for a myriad of reasons. Graduate students who see their contemporaries earning high salaries or enjoying their leisure time decide that they would prefer to do the same. For graduate students who become parents, their new family responsibilities increase the attraction of other lines of work that have more immediate and tangible satisfactions. Graduate students whose advisors ignore them or treat them poorly may conclude that they do not wish to participate in such an inhumane profession. Students suffering from medical problems, including psychological disorders like depression, may benefit from taking a leave of absence to deal with their illnesses instead of quitting altogether.

Once someone leaves a graduate program, it is indeed hard

to return. The good news is that, according to Susan Basalla and Maggie Debelius, who interviewed hundreds of former graduate students about their decisions to find "postacademic" careers, none regretted leaving the academy. They put their innate talents and acquired skills to work in all sorts of unexpected and often surprisingly gratifying ways. Many also kept up their academic interests in their spare time.[5]

Why do graduate students' personalities sometimes change?

Graduate study necessarily turns a student inward, causing her to learn as much about herself—how she works best, what she cares passionately about—as about the subject formally under study. This knowledge may alter a student's personality or behavior for good or ill.

Graduate students' personalities may change in at least three major ways. First, the intellectual field disciplines how a graduate student sees the world. Study in the humanities or social sciences may cause a student to understand economic inequality or social structures that were previously masked. Students in the sciences may sit around contemplating the chemistry or ecology of Thanksgiving dinner, where their relatives see just turkey. Sometimes the behavior exhibited by a student who is learning new ways of seeing the world is less a brand-new characteristic than an exaggeration of the traits that prompted the student to apply to graduate school in the first place. On the plus side, the new understandings of the world generated by graduate studies can undergird a person's politics with useful empirical evidence, provide fodder for fascinating discussions of how the world works, or help her to find a more humane interpretation of her personal relationships.

Secondly, graduate school has a tendency to exaggerate students' insecurities. Students typically receive from faculty members an unrelenting torrent of criticism. This can be a shock even to someone with the thickest skin and may be devastating to a student with unrealistic or unhealthy expectations for herself. Professors deliver critiques of students' work in order to help them think more clearly and become better scholars, but in the absence of mitigating praise, students may begin to doubt their basic abilities and intellectual fitness. "Imposter syndrome" is a shorthand for the commonplace feeling among academics that they have been mistakenly accepted into a fold they are not smart enough for. Alternatively, professors may simply fail to provide any feedback, suggesting to a student that her work is not worth sustained attention. Additionally, a student who felt herself to be a star at the undergraduate level may be demoralized by the realization that she is just average among her peers. All of these concerns can prompt graduate students to doubt themselves, worry, complain, and act cranky.

Finally, some students use their work as a convenient reason for not dealing with their personal issues, running off to the library or the lab to avoid a conflict with a romantic partner, roommate, friend, or parent. Like other stressful experiences, graduate school has the capacity to bring out the worst of a student's personality and

---

EXPERT TIP:

Some changes in personality and self-expression are perfectly natural by-products of graduate study. But in some cases, graduate school can bring to light mental health problems such as depression. A 2004 study of graduate students' mental health at one institution found that "almost half (44.7%) of the respondents reported having an emotional or stress-related problem over the previous year." A similar study of graduate students at the University of California at Berkeley found that, "67 percent of graduate students said that they had felt hopeless at least once in the past year. 54 percent felt so depressed they had a hard time functioning, and nearly 10 percent said they had considered suicide. . . . By comparison, an estimated 9.5 percent of American adults suffered from depressive disorders in a given year, according the National Institute of Mental Health." If you are worried about your own mental health or that of someone you care for, by all means, seek advice from a professional in the field such as a family doctor or the psychologists available at the campus health clinic.

---

provides an ironclad excuse to put off dealing with other problems indefinitely.

Why do graduate students often seem self-absorbed?

Graduate study is not just learning the content and analytic skills of the discipline; it is also learning about oneself. In part because graduate study has to be so self-directed, graduate students learn about themselves as they proceed through their programs—they learn what they are truly interested in and bored by; what routines and rituals help and hinder their work; where their passions lie; and whether they are really committed to the career they intended when they applied to graduate school. Such self-analysis is often valorized by graduate student subcultures. As a result, graduate students spend a lot of time basking in themselves, gazing at their belly buttons even more attentively than their mothers did when they were newborns.

Moreover, the only person who can do a graduate student's work is that student. In contrast to much of the work world, there are few teams to lean on in graduate school. Even scientists, who work in laboratories with other scientists and usually publish collaboratively, still have to do their own coursework and write their own dissertations. If the student intends to graduate, he has to be the one to do the work. The dependence on oneself alone can prompt a graduate student to behave unreasonably, even selfishly.

For some graduate students, asking them to take a day off is the equivalent of asking them to push their already elusive graduation date off further into the distance. Someone who is feeling generally good about himself might recognize a day off or even a week's vacation as refreshing, but someone already buckling under the strains of an unfinished thesis might regard that innocent request as a malicious effort to keep him from graduating.

Finally, balancing one's own needs with those of others can be particularly difficult for graduate students who are not proficient at

VOICE:

Graduate studies touch every aspect of my life. It is more than a full-time job, more than school, and more important than both. I never stop thinking about my topic, my deadlines, the impression I am making on my committee, fellow students, and colleagues. I even dream about it. How well I'm progressing on my dissertation affects my mood, every minute of my day. Also, a typical day for me is that I have to focus and think critically and express my thoughts on paper for at least 12 hours a day. I don't know of any other job that requires a person to be "on" that intensely.

—Ph.D. student, public health

VOICE:

Even when a person does have time for non-academic activities, I feel that I am not making productive use of my time unless I'm working on school-related work. Not that I feel guilty for every fun thing I do—I'm far from that—but I always have to convince myself that it's OK to take a break from studying.

—M.A. student, history

multitasking. Although the thesis or dissertation is only one task, it can loom so large in a person's life that he feels he has no room for any distractions—entertainment, friends, family, romance, exercise, food, or sleep. Workers with paid sick leave sometimes take a "mental health day" to enjoy themselves and get away from their offices. Employers may frown on this, but employees persist in the practice. Because graduate students are both their own employers and their own staff, the need for time off cuts both ways.

How can intellectual work take a physical toll on graduate students?

Like other people who suffer from stress, graduate students sometimes end up sick or laid low by other unexpected ailments. Little research has been conducted to ascertain how healthy graduate students are compared with peers of the same age. One study of graduate students of physical therapy—people who could reasonably be expected to appreciate the importance of exercise—found that women's body fat (but not men's) increased during their schooling. The study argued that students should be given more time to ensure their physical fitness.[6] Because the time demands of graduate school are endless, graduate students need to make special efforts to protect their well-being.

Except for those whose research requires physical fitness, like field geologists or biologists, graduate students' labor can best be described as sedentary. Long hours in the library, the infinite stack of work, and feelings of guilt about doing anything other than studying often mean that graduate students simply do not get the exercise that a healthy person needs. Graduate students can push their eyes and brains too hard, so that focused reading, late nights, odd hours, and too much caffeine create eyestrain and headaches. Additionally, graduate students are vulnerable to the kinds of injuries common to other office workers, such as carpal tunnel syndrome. Finally, the psychological stress of graduate school can exacerbate physical ailments and make recovery difficult.

How long does graduate school take?

When a college student in the United States enrolls in an undergraduate program, the reasonable expectation is that with full-time study she can complete the degree in four years. Many students do take longer, especially if they are enrolled only part-time. The norm for graduate education is that a master's degree should take two or three years and a doctoral degree five.

How long a student's program actually takes varies considerably. Where an undergraduate degree is earned through the completion of a foreordained number of classes that are contained within the structure of a quarter or a semester, most graduate degrees require both coursework and independent research. A student's coursework can be completed in lockstep with his cohort, but how long the independent research takes depends on the student's work ethic, success in defining a manageable project, luck in the execution of the research, and the timeliness of his advisor's response to his writing. All of these factors can extend the time to degree well beyond the "normal" three or five years of study. Only a few programs take seriously the responsibility to push their students out in a short time frame.

Why is five years considered the normal amount of time it takes to complete a doctorate?

In the ideal model in the twenty-first century, it takes five years to complete a doctorate. The first two years are for coursework; the third year for exams and preparing a dissertation proposal; the fourth year is for researching the dissertation; the final year for writing. Universities sometimes enforce the desirability of this premise; they may support graduate students financially through a fifth year with teaching assistantships and fellowships, but after that they become punitive. Some universities cut off advanced students' access to the library, threaten to dismiss slow dissertators, or provide other incentives to encourage students to finish their degrees.

The five-year model, however, has little relationship to reality. Since the 1970s, the "time to degree" has been steadily increasing. Students tend to finish doctorates in the sciences faster than in the humanities, but times are increasing across the disciplines. Time spent teaching, the necessity of supporting oneself once university funding dries up, the prospect of building a family, and the increasing pressure on graduate students to publish (as a way of building a CV that will attract the attention of a tenure-track search committee) all slow down graduate students.[7] Nettles and Millett's recent survey of more than 9,000 doctoral students found that the mean time to complete a degree was 5.97 years. Engineers worked quickly

EXPERT TIP:

Dissertation advisors can make or break careers. A student provided with sensible suggestions about choosing a topic, constructive criticism as the project proceeds, polite but insistent urging to finish, and encouragement throughout, should, working full time, be able to complete the dissertation in less than two years and possibly closer to one. But given an inept or irresponsible advisor, a student can become like Tantalus, condemned to watch the object of desire recede at every attempt to attain it.

—Steven M. Cahn, *Saints and Scamps*

at 5.23 years, with students in mathematics coming in at 4.71 years. Students in the social sciences took 6.35 years to complete their degrees, and those in the humanities took 7.41 years.[8] Even competitive fellowship programs that funded graduate students to focus exclusively on their research did not speed them up.[9] Several well-funded efforts, such as the Andrew W. Mellon Foundation's Graduate Education Initiative, have recently explored ways to check the propensity for growth in time to degree, with only moderate success.

Many graduate students cannot predict when they will finish their research or writing. Laboratory scientists whose projects are part of a larger effort coordinated by their advisor rely on that professor to tell them when they have completed enough research and written enough articles that they are ready to defend a dissertation. Archive-dependent students cannot know how long it will take them to read (or photocopy) their way through their primary sources. In fields where students come to understand their research only through the process of writing it up, the amount of time it will take to compose the dissertation is unpredictable; indeed, for all graduate students, who almost certainly are doing a thesis or dissertation for the first time, how long it takes to complete that massive independent project is unknowable. Unless the advisor is keeping close tabs on the student and tells him when he has enough material, a student may well do much more research than is strictly necessary to complete the dissertation. Even then, a student may not heed the advice. I distinctly recall that my advisor told me I had enough research for a dissertation before I felt ready to write; for months thereafter I snuck out to the archives without telling him. He was right, though. More than a decade later I am still publishing from research I initiated as part of my dissertation.

What are residency requirements?

Universities often have "residency requirements" that compel graduate students to be on campus for a certain stretch of time during their studies. Such rules require a student to be enrolled for a specified number of courses over a particular number of semesters, usually sequentially. Summer classes often do not count toward residency requirements. The purpose of such requirements is to ensure that students are immersed in the academic milieu and connected to a community of classmates. The premise of this policy is that graduate school is more than just a series of courses followed by a thesis; rather, graduate school is an immersion experience greater than the sum of its parts.

For full-time graduate students, especially those working as teaching or research assistants or supported by fellowships, fulfilling residency requirements is so natural they may not even be aware of the regulations. For part-time students, especially those with outside work or childcare responsibilities, fulfilling residency requirements and can be onerous and even undermine their basic intent. The student must find a series of semesters in which she can be continuously enrolled in appropriate classes. Graduate students fulfilling residency requirements and juggling other responsibilities may feel particularly stressed during this time.

What are time limits?

Some graduate programs and universities put time limits on the degree: unless a student fulfills all requirements within the time limits, the degree will not be granted. Master's students typically have five years to complete their programs; Ph.D. students have ten or twelve years. Students who wish to complete their degrees after the limits expire may be forced to jump through various extra hoops to confirm their seriousness. A student who has withdrawn from the program before reaching ABD status might have to reapply for admission to his original program. An ABD student whose writing extends beyond the time limits might be required to retake the preliminary exams before being granted the Ph.D., even if her committee members are happy (even relieved) to accept the finished dissertation.

The rationale for time limits is that, after a certain point, the student's familiarity with the relevant scholarly literature—the currency of the realm—becomes stale. Graduate-level independent work represents the cutting edge of knowledge. Dissertations and theses rooted in works read in the distant past are less likely to reflect the current scholarship. In fast-moving fields such as computer science, reliance on five-year-old scholarly literature might make a dissertation outdated the moment it is finished. As a practical matter, a student who stretches out the time to finish his degree may find that the faculty members with whom he took classes and planned to have on his thesis committee are no longer around; assembling a committee when a student no longer knows the faculty can be exceptionally difficult. Some institutions, however, reject the notion of time limits and will graduate a student whenever he completes the requirements.

Is there a best approach to getting through graduate school?

The short answer: No.

A longer answer: Some people think so, but I do not.

The most efficient graduate students often take the following approach: they start graduate school with a dissertation or thesis topic in mind and make sure that every paper they write, for every class, contributes to the dissertation. If they have to write a literature review, then they do a literature review on the anticipated dissertation topic and use that literature review as a chapter in the thesis. If they have to conduct original research for classes, then they figure out how to apportion the dissertation research into smaller packages and investigate one for each research-oriented class. If a professor assigns a dissertation proposal, these efficiency buffs make sure that the paper and the dissertation's needs match.

It turns out, however, that this approach does not work for everyone—even for people who are fine scholars. Some students do not enter graduate school with a laser-like focus on their dissertations. Some cannot hone in on a topic immediately because they are new to their discipline; others know that they love the field but have not yet figured out what area of research interests them most. Others' interests change as they explore the intellectual landscapes. Some scholars simply prefer not to work in a linear fashion, and such people benefit from casting their nets broadly, learning about diverse topics and methods before settling on a narrow thesis topic.

Even people with advanced degrees in their fields are rarely excellent at all aspects of their chosen discipline. Some people are intuitive researchers; others are just dogged. Some people have flashes of insight that generate discipline-shifting ideas; others are better at sniffing out gaps in knowledge and filling in those gaps. Some scholars find writing the easiest part of producing a disserta-

---

EXPERT TIP:
One of my professors—a giant in our field—repeatedly told his doctoral students, "Write down your ideas on little scraps of paper and keep them in your pockets." That advice had clearly served him well—he had purchased a vacation home with the royalties from his landmark book. But I knew that I would never be able to keep track of ideas that ended up in the washing machine before I managed to file them. Graduate students certainly should find out what has worked for other scholars and experiment based on the advice of successful models but also feel free to discard approaches that seem unnatural.

tion; others labor over every word. Some academics thrive when they know everything about a given topic; others learn enough to satisfy their curiosity and then move on to greener pastures. Different approaches to research serve these various intellectual styles differently. A significant but usually completely unspoken part of the graduate school agenda is discovering what research and writing style works best for the individual student. Graduate school is a voyage of discovery—not just of the discipline and thesis topic, but of the student's own best research, thinking, and writing processes.

CHAPTER 4

Coursework Is Hard Work

A s the director of a graduate program that attracts many nontraditional students, I meet many students who have been out of college for decades or have never known anyone who has earned a graduate degree. Much of my job involves interpreting to my students academic culture at large, as well as our specific program. Recently, as a new student sat in my office, I asked him how he was doing in the program. He said that it was "not too bad," as he was not "failing" any of his classes. Having gathered intelligence from my colleagues that seemed to contradict what he was saying, I pressed him for details. It transpired that in one of his classes, most of his papers were getting Cs. I had to explain to him, because no one else had thought to, that in graduate school a C is considered a warning that a student may not be fit for graduate study; that essentially it is a failing grade.

The early years of graduate school offer a strange mixture: on the one hand, beginning graduate students are novices, taking classes like undergraduates and unfamiliar with local routines. On the other hand, they are apprentice scholars, sometimes in positions of authority over students, and are expected to contribute to the intellectual life of senior faculty. Many of the academic routines that graduate students encounter are unique to the experience of graduate study. No counterparts exist at the undergraduate level, and once a student leaves graduate school, she will never encounter such hurdles again—unless she takes a job as a professor and must administer them herself. This chapter looks at what beginning graduate students have to understand about their work, in addition to the contents of their classes.

What are the steps in obtaining a graduate degree?

Obtaining a *master's* degree is usually a two-stage process. The first step is completing a body of required coursework, typically a core of content and methodological courses and a relatively small number of elective courses that are somehow relevant to the discipline. The second step is usually an exit exercise; either an exam or a thesis. Students who complete a thesis successfully demonstrate their ability to conduct original research in the discipline and therefore signal their capacity to study at the doctoral level. Students who choose not to do a thesis but take an exam or other such exercise are, in effect, earning a "terminal" master's degree and acknowledging that they will not continue on to the Ph.D. Admissions committees at the doctoral level rarely decide to accept someone who completed a master's degree without conducting a major piece of original research and writing.

Earning a *Ph.D.* is more complicated. Like the master's degree, doctoral study typically begins with a defined body of coursework, including content areas, methods, and electives. Students in the humanities sometimes must demonstrate mastery of a foreign language, which they may have to study on top of required courses in their major field. Students may also be encouraged or required to pursue a minor in a related field. Upon completing their coursework, doctoral students usually have to pass an exam or set of exams that demonstrate their mastery of the scholarly literature in their field or basic competence in important research techniques. Having passed the exam, the student may now refer to herself as a dissertator, or ABD ("all but dissertation"; that is, someone who has done almost everything required for the doctorate). The next step is usually the preparation of a dissertation proposal, a plan for the project that the student intends to conduct during the balance of her formal education. Finally, the student researches, writes, and orally defends the dissertation.

What kinds of courses do graduate students take?

In some respects, the menu of graduate courses resembles an advanced version of an undergraduate major—a mix of methods and content courses, without general education requirements or scads of electives. But while undergraduate majors are structured to provide students with a survey of their field, graduate degrees are much more specialized. The authors of *The Ph.D. Process* point out that "nowadays, students could not receive an exhaustive, general education in their fields if they were given a lifetime to try."[1] So, graduate students usually concentrate on one or two subfields within their larger discipline. In addition, graduate programs often require students to take "methods courses," which introduce students to the approaches to research shared by most practitioners of a discipline, regardless of the content area of their expertise. Because graduate training is so specialized, people with advanced degrees often know very little about other subfields of their own discipline unless they have formally studied or made a concerted effort to read into them. Sometimes graduate students pursue a minor field, either within

EXPERT TIP:
One useful exercise for a new student is to try to describe the larger landscape and organization of his discipline for a friend. What areas will he become expert in and what areas remain mysterious? For example, both sociology and psychology have subfields called "social psychology." If he is studying one of these areas, explain to the friend how it differs from its namesake. Sometimes the subfields have names that sound funny to outsiders. A major category of mathematics, for example, is "Algebra." Although that sounds like a topic studied in junior high school, it is not! Being able to talk about where one's work fits into the larger scheme of ideas can help graduate students understand the future path of their research and persuade colleagues that they are broadly intellectually curious people worth being around.

their departments or in allied fields. The minor field may enhance their research skills or represent an extra teaching area.

How important are letter grades or GPA in graduate school?

Grades in particular classes matter a little, but a student's grade point average (GPA) matters almost not at all. Grades are significant in that they show roughly how a student's coursework is proceeding, and in some programs, funding decisions take into consideration student GPA rankings. In the long run, though, no one will ever care about a graduate's GPA or whether she got an A or a B in a particular course unless she is applying for admission to study for a new graduate or professional degree.

Everyone who is in graduate school did not get straight As as undergraduates, but they had to do fairly well to be accepted into a graduate program. Lower-tier graduate institutions often have minimum GPA requirements for applicants. Those minima may apply to the entire undergraduate coursework, not just to the relevant major. Students with lower GPAs are either rejected outright or admitted into graduate school on probation; if their grades in their first few semesters of graduate school are not high enough, they can be kicked out of their programs.

However, a good-enough grade for an undergraduate is not necessarily enough for a graduate student. A grades remain the ceiling, but the floor is much higher than the traditional A

> **EXPERT TIP:**
> It is not necessary to obsess over grades; after you successfully complete a course, *it is unlikely that anyone will ever ask what grade you received.*
>
> —Bloom, Karp, and Cohen, *The Ph.D. Process*

> **VOICE:**
> "Passing" = A-level work at a graduate school level. A B+ in a class put your funding in jeopardy in my world. Anything less than a B+ = please reconsider your time here. A "C" = you were unceremoniously booted without warning.
>
> —Iomhaigh, re "Why is grad school so hard?"

VOICE:

Partly because of the ridiculous grading system now in place in most graduate programs, according to which a "B" equals an "F," students have a hard time understanding what constitutes exceptional or mediocre or subpar work.

—Gregory M. Colón Semenza, *Graduate Study for the Twenty-First Century*

VOICE:

One department head ... asked to justify the extraordinarily high percentage of A's given by his department, replied confidently: "That's no problem. Our students always know when they don't do well. We make it obvious with an A–."

—Steven M. Cahn, *Saints and Scamps*

to F scale. Professors grade graduate students' work to underscore the idea that professors grade *work*, not people. In most cases, the only grades that are given to graduate students are As and Bs (perhaps with pluses and minuses). As a result, graduate students often have an inflated sense of their own status. The authors of *Three Magic Letters* discovered that "approximately 45 percent of all doctoral students rated themselves in the top 10 percent, and another 34 percent situated their performance in the top 25 percent."[2] In many doctoral programs, they explain, "grades are typically taken lightly as objective indicators of the quality of student performance, since most doctoral students earn an A in every course, making it difficult to distinguish between high achievers and average achievers."[3] This narrow range makes a B the lowest of the passing grades. What if a student earns too many B minuses? The university may put the student on academic probation, a warning that he will be expelled if he does not bring his grades up. Anything in the C range is a message that the student has, essentially, failed the assignment or course. Below a C? A signal that the student has not completed the required work or has committed some sort of academic fraud. More than one C in a class? The student should consider quitting, if the school has not already kicked him out.

Faculty search committees do not compare job candidates' GPAs in order to decide whom to hire. Their decisions are based on the quality of a candidate's research and pedagogy. Occasionally colleges or universities hiring new faculty request a transcript from job applicants, but the main purpose of such inquiry is to make sure that potential employees have not falsified their credentials.

How important is research during the coursework years?

The central purpose of graduate programs is to create scholars who are capable of conceptualizing lines of inquiry and executing research projects that lead to new knowledge. Learning how to conduct research is *the* crucial skill that graduate students apply themselves to. Where this learning occurs, however, varies by discipline. In the sciences, where graduate students are funded to begin conducting their advisors' projects, most work on original research as soon as they start. That research is directed within the context of a laboratory and supervised by a PI who intends to publish the results of their work. Classwork for these students is almost ancillary, a necessary but subsidiary activity that is the only excuse for being absent from the bench. In the social sciences and humanities, students learn to conduct research primarily within the context of their classes, which professors structure to allow students to learn the skills and topics they will need to complete their independent projects successfully. Class papers can often be incorporated directly into exam papers or the thesis.

VOICE:

Graduate students have been granted a special favor. They have been allowed to pursue their fantasies. They are given the freedom to explore how nature operates, and they do so through the eyes and ears and minds of the most sophisticated instruments and technologies mankind has to offer. Commanding these powerful tools, they ask interesting questions and get interesting answers. Money is provided for them, so that supplies can be bought and experiments conducted.

—Bloom, Karp, and Cohen, *The Ph.D. Process*

How does graduate coursework help a student write a thesis?

Graduate coursework can help students prepare to write their theses in three different ways. In some cases, a class provides students with specific intellectual content needed to pursue a particular project. This knowledge might include a review of relevant scholarly literature, coverage of an important research technique, or background information essential to the student's thesis topic. In addition, all graduate courses (in theory, anyway) contribute to a student's general intellectual growth, introducing her to new ideas and important professional standards. While such development does not translate directly into a thesis project, it readies a student to understand the parameters for formulating, executing, and completing an independent project.

Finally, graduate coursework may well provide direct inspiration for a thesis project. By reading broadly in the discipline and talking with peers and professors, students figure out what is exciting, new, interesting, and still undiscovered in their fields. Something as small as a single, unexpected sentence in an optional reading might spark a student to think of an entirely new line of inquiry—a promising route to finding a thesis topic.

How should a student use coursework to prepare for writing a thesis or dissertation?

There are two philosophies about how to use coursework to prepare for a thesis or dissertation. The first approach, which is surely the more practical of the two, is to pick a thesis topic early in one's graduate career and make sure that every paper written for every class can also serve as a piece of the thesis. Doing this on a systematic basis will mean that a student can start the dissertation writing process with as much as one-half of the thesis already in draft form, requiring only editing to be consistent with subsequent research.

The other approach is to wander through a variety of courses writing papers on whatever topics seem compelling within the context of the class. The student who takes this approach may not have a dissertation topic spelled out when the time to write a proposal rolls around, but she still has built important skills required for independent research and will have learned about a broader variety of topics than her more focused counterpart.

Which approach is better? It depends on the student's personality and goals. Some are interested in learning as much information about as many topics as possible; others have a laser-like intensity and put a premium on earning the degree quickly. Students who are in graduate school because they love to learn and cannot imagine what else could be as much fun probably are better served by the peripatetic approach. Students who need a degree for career advancement and do not find graduate school intrinsically rewarding ought to focus on expeditiously meeting all requirements, including the thesis. These differences also apply to students who are pursing Ph.D.s with the goal of a being a college professor. Someone who aspires to a job at a school oriented toward teaching, such as a small liberal arts college or a community college, should learn about many different topics on the way to the dissertation, because most of his teaching assignments will be broad courses at the introductory level. A student who wants to teach at a prestigious, research-oriented university probably should amass as much knowledge as possible about a narrow topic, with the goal of producing the kind of deeply researched, sophisticated, innovative dissertation that will attract the attention of faculty search committees at such institutions.

What are comps, quals, prelims, generals, cumes, and orals?

In short, they are exams. Most doctoral programs require students to pass some sort of examination either during coursework or shortly after it is finished. Some master's programs do this as well.

The specific purpose of the exam—for most students a stress-inducing experience—varies with the discipline and the program, but the general goal of such a test is to make sure that the student understands the field well enough to conduct independent research. In some cases, students are tested on their understanding of a specific reading list dictated by faculty; in others, students develop a personalized bibliography. These tests of knowledge and analytic skill are often followed by oral exams that rate a student's professional demeanor: how do they handle questions whose answers they simply do not know? (Not coincidentally, this is an essential skill for college professors.) Such exams must be passed in order to qualify for the next step of the program (such as writing a thesis) or graduating and are not subject to the kind of continuous, improvement-oriented critique that theses are.

Exams may be offered on a timetable set by the program or at the convenience of the student and supervising faculty members. Students sit for some exams for a fixed number of hours in a supervised room without outside resources; other exams allot weeks or even months for the writing process. Many of these exams have two components: a written portion followed shortly thereafter by an oral exam; other exams consist only of one or the other. Regardless of the structure of the exam, observe the authors of *The Ph.D. Process*, "all require the ability to remember, assimilate, synthesize, and integrate a vast amount of material."[4]

Grading tends to be on a pass/fail basis. Some institutions offer a "pass with distinction" to students who perform particularly well. Most programs allow a student who fails to retake the exam, once. In cases of multiple failures, students may be involuntarily terminated from their programs. In certain circumstances, the university or program imposes a finish-by date on the student's achievement in order to foster freshness of the material; if the dissertation is not completed within a specified time frame (often five to seven years) following the exam, the student with a completed dissertation who hopes to graduate must retake and repass the exam before receiving a diploma.

What follows are general descriptions of the kinds of exams, rather than absolute definitions. What looks like a comp in one program might be called a prelim in another. Some programs require students to pass multiple exams of different types before graduating.

Qualifying exams are also known as quals. They appear frequently in the sciences and mathematics and test whether the student has mastered a broad spectrum of either undergraduate or elementary graduate-level knowledge. Qualifying exams tend to be administered early in the student's graduate career, during the first year or the beginning of the second, usually at a time fixed by the program.

Cumes (rhymes with rooms) is short for cumulative exams, which test what a student knows about the subfields of her discipline. Like qualifying exams, cumulative exams test specific knowledge and the student's ability to apply that knowledge to the kinds of unexpected circumstances that arise in the process of doing original research. Cumes, too, must be passed relatively early in a program.

Comps, short for comprehensive exams, are tests of the student's broad knowledge of the subject matter of coursework required in the program. The assumption guiding comprehensive exams is that to be a master or doctor of a field, one must actually know about the broad shape of the field.

A *general exam*, despite its name, is often a test of whether the student is prepared to begin original research in his chosen field of specialization. Sometimes a general exam more closely resembles a cumulative exam in that it is a test of a student's knowledge of a subfield within the degree program.

Prelim is short for preliminary examination. As the term implies, the prelim is a hurdle, a prerequisite to the dissertation. In order to write a satisfactory dissertation, a student needs to be able to say how his original research advances the state of the field, which he cannot do without being able to articulate the state of the field. Therefore, the preliminary examination tests what the student knows about other scholars' research and how the various arguments in the field relate. Prelim exams are especially likely to consist of long papers, sometimes expected to be of publishable quality, written over a relatively long period of time.

Orals may refer either to an exam administered solely through a live interrogation or to the second portion of an exam that follows on successful completion of a written test. Orals may also refer to the oral defense of a completed dissertation or thesis. In the British university system, students refer to an oral by its Latin name *viva voce*, or just *viva*.

Why do graduate students in many fields, even the sciences, have to pass foreign-language exams?

Once upon a time in the history of American scholarship, the universe of knowledge and ideas available in English was small. In order to be conversant with cutting-edge ideas in most disciplines, a scholar needed to know several foreign languages, especially

German, French, and Latin. The requirement that students demonstrate competence in at least one foreign language is a relic of this tradition.

Advanced-degree programs derive some sense that they are turning out truly educated professionals if their students can read in a language other than English. Faculty also argue that learning another language requires students to stretch intellectually in a way that is vital and cannot be attained by any other means. Of course, some research areas really do necessitate fluency in foreign languages: an anthropologist cannot hope to understand how Russians use the Internet without knowing Russian. But language requirements often extend far beyond what is strictly justified by the need for research.

What is an advisor?

An advisor is a member of a program's graduate faculty who directs a student's studies. Students new to graduate school may be assigned an advisor, more or less arbitrarily. Early in graduate school, the advisor's main job is to help the student figure out which courses to take and how to navigate the larger institution. But advanced students generally seek out advisors whose research methodologies and interests they share. In the later stages of graduate school, the advisor's major responsibilities are to supervise the student's research and aid him in seeking a postgraduation academic job.

At a minimum, the advisor's job involves reading and critiquing the student's scholarship. Peter Feibelman observes that "scientists are like terriers, trained to chase down and pick apart reasoning that is not rigorous,"[5] and he could just as well have been referring to advisors worth their salt in any discipline. The tone of critique may seem hostile or friendly, depending on the advisor's personality, but the intent of scholarly criticism is always to improve the work.

What makes a good advisor?

A good advisor is someone who helps the student in the ways she needs to be helped. Sometimes a good advisor can annoy a student; for example, she might demand better research or analysis than the student is inclined to do when left to her own devices. But by and large a good advisor considers a student's personality as well as intellectual capacities when giving counsel. The basic goal of a good advisor is to see a student through to a successful completion of graduate studies. Some graduate advisors extend their efforts on behalf of their students well beyond graduation, helping them to find jobs, make connections in the discipline, and publish their early scholarship. The best advisors understand their students as people, not just as research machines, giving them permission to take down time when life demands it.

When should a student get an advisor?

Some students enter their graduate programs with their advising relationships already defined. The application process requires them to state whom they want to study under, and they are admitted only if the advisor commits to supervising them. Other programs initially offer new students the advisory services of a director of graduate studies. Students are expected to get to know the faculty in the first year or two of their program and thus find someone with the appropriate expertise and personality fit.

Asking an advisor to take a student on can be harrowing. One friend of mine baked for her professor, an internationally famous scholar, until he agreed to supervise her food-oriented dissertation. To cite my own case, I kept going back to my advisor's office without ever formally asking him to take me on. One student of mine asked me if I would supervise his thesis and then commented that it was harder than, but not unlike, asking someone for a date. However the relationship is formed, students cannot do their independent work without an advisor.

Can graduate students change advisors?

Yes. Graduate students can and do change advisors. Sometimes the reasons are intellectual. Students' interests evolve with their studies and it may turn out that the person they had planned to work with is no longer the best-qualified to advise their research. In other cases, the reasons for breaking up with an advisor are intensely personal. An advisor may turn out to be a bad personal match for a given student. Some advisors give their advisees so little attention that the student concludes that to succeed she must locate a new mentor. Faculty members, for their part, have been known to drop advisees who do not live up to their standards.

Changing advisors, however, can be politically tricky. An advisor who derives prestige from the number or quality of her advisees may attempt to sabotage a new dyad, resenting the departing student for perceived disloyalty or distrusting his colleague for having poached. On the other hand, a student may hope to keep the former advisor on the dissertation committee. Finding a way to "demote" the advisor without destroying the basic relationship requires tact. A more complex difficulty is presented when students are dependent on their advisors for funding: to find a new major professor, they may have to be accepted into a new lab as well.

What happens if an advisor leaves the university where the graduate student is studying?

Because the relationship between the advisor and the graduate student is so important, the departure of the faculty member from the university can cause upheaval in the life of a doctoral student. Yet faculty members do sometimes leave their jobs: assistant professors are denied tenure or move to other institutions, and while more senior faculty leave less frequently, they still do occasionally take other opportunities, leaving for a year or permanently or in the worst cases becoming unavailable through incapacity or death.

When an advisor moves to a new university, his Ph.D. students may have the option of following him to the new school. Unless they are denied tenure, teach in a toxic department, or have family constraints, faculty rarely accept new positions where they have less opportunity to teach graduate students. Training graduate students generally carries prestige, and to leave a department with a graduate program for one with only undergraduate teaching is understood as a demotion in status. Students of a faculty member who is transferring make formal applications to the new program, and given their advisor's endorsement they have a high probability of acceptance. Whether they also receive comparable funding at the new institution is an open question, depending largely on the advisor's clout and grants. In such cases, students may receive credit for coursework completed in the original doctoral program but still have to meet certain requirements of the new one.

For some students, however, moving with an advisor is not an attractive option. Students who have chosen a particular graduate program for its proximity to family or other commitments might prefer to stay in the original program and find a new advisor, even if this means shifting their research focus. A student who is far into the dissertation-writing process may prefer to find a new professor who will formally head the committee, while keeping the former advisor on as a consultant or "outside reader." However, the earlier in a program a student is, the easier it is to start over at a new school with the old advisor.

Master's students, whose programs are shorter and less dependent on a single individual, are much less likely to shift institutions with an advisor.

CHAPTER 5

Dissertations and Theses

···

Sitting in an airport once, I struck up a conversation with a woman who turned out to be a nun, a Ph.D., and a professor of mathematics at a local university. I was most impressed by her story about her dissertation. While she was still taking graduate classes, she wrote a paper that was so original that her professor told her she had just finished her dissertation. She still had several classes to take and she had yet to pass her exams, but after completing those hurdles all she needed to do was to package her class paper according to university regulations and she could receive her doctorate.

Most graduate students do not accidentally write their dissertations. Norms for how students complete their projects vary by field. In some areas, the student's plans for the dissertation, as outlined in a dissertation proposal, constitute the first several chapters of the final product. In scientific areas, graduate students routinely publish several chapters of their work in scholarly journals, then add an introduction and conclusion that tie them together and call that a dissertation. In still other fields, a student's plans evolve on the fly, making the final dissertation entirely different from its appearance as first imagined. When I cleaned out my car recently—a car I am still driving well into its second decade—I was intrigued to find a draft page from my dissertation proposal. It imagined a project that looked almost nothing like the dissertation I ended up writing. The central concerns and locale were the same, but the people and period under study were entirely different. This chapter reviews the final hurdle in the process of obtaining a graduate degree—conducting a full-scale, independent, original project.

What is a thesis?

A thesis is an original scholarly project that demonstrates the student's ability to conduct research independently. Theses are generally shorter and more modest in scope and ambition than doctoral dissertations. Master's theses may or may not be cataloged in a university library and are not easily accessible to scholars at other institutions who might be interested in their contents.

Many, but not all, master's level programs require a thesis for graduation. In some programs, a thesis is optional. By and large, a master's student who plans continued study in a Ph.D. program should write a thesis. If a student opts out of writing a thesis, it suggests to Ph.D. admissions committees that she is not serious enough about research to write a doctoral dissertation. After all, if a thesis is a minidissertation, how could someone who could not write a thesis hope to complete the more rigorous requirements of the dissertation? For this reason, a master's degree without a thesis is generally considered a terminal master's.

Sometimes the word *thesis* is shorthand for *dissertation*. To add a layer of confusion, *thesis* can also refer to the main argument within any work of scholarship, whether it is a paper, a thesis, a dissertation, an article, or a book. But the word *dissertation* is clear: it is reserved for the capstone of the work for the doctorate.

What is a dissertation?

A dissertation is the culmination of the work for the doctorate. It is a substantial, original research project, planned, executed, and written by the student himself. It is almost universally expected that dissertation research should be of interest to at least a few scholars in the same discipline. Dissertations are cataloged by uni-

Graduate students are generally careful to distinguish between a "paper" and their thesis or dissertation, feeling that reducing a multiyear research project to a class paper (which under some circumstances can be written in an hour or two) slights both their work and them personally.

VOICE:
You know that feeling you get when you find the perfect source for the perfect undergrad paper that you will write perfectly, and get a perfect "A" on? Well, in grad school, we're being trained to write that perfect source. It's a whole other beast.

—Grasshopper, re "Why is grad school so hard?"

VOICE:
But the Diss[ertation] has become (and perhaps needs to be for a while) *a calling, an object of some measure of daily devotion*—from the mind, the heart, perhaps the soul (altho in a good way).

—Rosamunde, "I saw a play today!"

versity libraries and other abstracting bibliographic services so that scholars at other institutions can locate and obtain them, even if they do not personally know the author.

The standards describing how much research the student must conduct entirely on her own and how long the dissertation should be vary by discipline. In the sciences, for example, where students usually work in (and are paid by) the laboratories of their advisors, and where collaboration is standard, a student's dissertation project is normally a part of a larger investigation organized by the advisor. In some of the social sciences, it is possible to write a dissertation based on information extracted from a published dataset, in which someone with no particular connection to the student gathered the raw research material. The heart of this project is original analysis. In the humanities, it is more typical for a student to design, conduct, and write up a dissertation project entirely unrelated to the research being performed by the advisor or anyone else at the university.

The lengths of doctoral dissertations vary considerably. A dissertation in mathematics might be just a dozen pages long. A dissertation in English or comparative literature is more likely to be as long as a published book; it might even occupy two volumes. The range of dissertation lengths is suggestive of how the different disciplines express their ideas; there is no implication that, because it is short, a short physics dissertation is easy to write or that, because of its greater length, a history dissertation is more difficult.

Who reads dissertations?

Dissertations tend to be written for very small audiences. The only readers that a graduate student can count on are those who sit on her dissertation committee and therefore have to read it as part of their jobs (though many a graduate student has been known to complain of "lazy" committee members who did not bother to read their theses before the defense). Some graduate students are surprised to discover that anyone else might read their dissertations and are shocked when they receive royalty payments, should someone order a copy.

But the research conducted by graduate students can be invaluable to other scholars working in the same field. The audience of interested scholars may be small—totaling only a few people worldwide—but for that audience a dissertation on a topic of interest can be crucial. If a graduate student has already gone to the trouble of tracking down and interpreting obscure materials, then another scholar can save significant effort by reading the dissertation in-

> **EXPERT TIP:**
> Although graduate students write for experts, sometimes non-experts want to know about their work. Graduate students who are deeply enamored of their research are usually capable of waxing eloquently on the topic for hours, without noticing frantic cues from conversation partners that it is time to stop. Some, however, find the thesis or dissertation so stressful that they cannot talk to anyone about it. Graduate students entering the job market are routinely advised to develop a three-sentence answer to the question, "what is your dissertation about?" as a way of orienting potential colleagues to their research interests without boring them.

stead of duplicating the research. By and large, reading and deeply understanding a work of scholarship requires some knowledge of a field; dissertations tend to be harder to read than published works because they are written for a small audience and lack the benefits of professional editing. Some dissertations can easily be converted into publications of general interest, but others remain important only to research specialists.

How do I find out what is the cutting edge in my field?

One of the most useful pieces of information that a graduate student can cultivate is a big picture of his discipline. A scholar who understands the larger landscape of the state of knowledge in the field can articulate the importance of his narrow project. Being able to "tell your story," as Peter Feibelman puts it, relating a particular project to bigger concerns, makes any research presentation more compelling to an audience.[1] But how can a mere graduate student learn enough about the state of a field to contextualize his relatively small project? Talking with and listening to other scholars is the key to finding out the shape and trajectory of a field. Clues to the story of a discipline can be gleaned by regular reading of relevant journals and new books, attending seminars, journal clubs, public talks, and conferences, and by chatting with colleagues.

Should a graduate student try to work in a trendy area of research?

Using trendiness alone as a map to research is not the best strategy for a graduate student who wants to establish a professional career. Academic publishing is slow; sometimes it takes years for an idea to percolate its way from inception to publication. Something that becomes trendy may well have been in the works for a decade, meaning that anyone who picks up on the trend becomes a follower, not a pacesetter.

That said, there are solid reasons for working in areas that other scholars in the field recognize as legitimate and expanding, rather than moribund. Students who hope to leverage their graduate degrees into jobs should focus their research where their expertise will be valued. Few history departments, for example, set out to hire old-fashioned military historians any more, but a historian of the military who writes through a lens of gender or the environment may well find an academic home. In laboratory sciences, where the lab head sets the research agenda for lab participants, it is her responsibility to make sure that there will be scholarly venues for the lab's findings. The lab's PI should have her finger on the pulse of the discipline and know what will become fundable, publishable, and significant scholarship.

How much autonomy do graduate students have in choosing their research topics?

The amount of leeway that graduate students have to pick their research topics varies with their advisor and their source of funding. Students who work as research assistants in their advisor's laboratory choose projects subsidiary to the larger scholarly agenda set by the PI. Although independent-minded students may chafe, this approach is a win-win situation because it speeds the student's time to completion and facilitates speedy publication while at the same time advancing the PI's research program. A science graduate student who secures individual external funding may have more autonomy in choosing the direction of his dissertation research, but he must persuade his committee of the project's viability.

Students in the humanities and social sciences, who are much less likely to be funded as research assistants in larger projects, are less beholden to their advisors' research interests. The flip side of insecure funding is scope for defining the subject and parameters of one's own research. As long as a student can persuade her advisors that a project is feasible and her advisor agrees that he is competent to oversee it, almost anything within the field (subject to IRB approval if it involves human-subject research) is fair game. A few advisors do prefer to micromanage their students' careers and parcel out predefined topics to their students. The upside of such close supervision is that the student benefits from the advisor's wisdom and experience in defining successful projects; the downside is that she may be uninterested in the topic that is assigned.

Who evaluates a thesis or dissertation?

A thesis or dissertation committee is the group of faculty members who evaluate a graduate student's progress toward the degree. In particular, the job of "the committee" is to advise the research and to evaluate the final version of the master's thesis or doctoral dissertation. Committee members' responsibilities include suggesting promising avenues for research, holding a preliminary or other intermediate examination to determine the student's fitness for writing a dissertation, evaluating a thesis proposal, reading the thesis itself (sometimes in draft form), and finally attending a formal hearing to determine whether the student has passed the degree program's capstone exercise. Committee members often serve as counselors and references for students going on the job market or applying to further education programs.

Students usually have input into the composition of their committees. Typically, after consultation with his primary advisor, a student asks from two to four members of the faculty in his program if they will serve on his committee. In addition to considering the content and methodological expertise of potential committee members, students also usually consider how well the various personalities on the committee mesh. Putting professional enemies on the same committee risks having them yell at each other during meetings, offer conflicting directives for improvement, and hold the student's graduation as a hostage in their continuing war. Finding out about departmental politics ahead of time can be a key part of assembling a committee.

Most committee members are "graduate faculty" from the student's own degree program. (Graduate faculty are the subset of university faculty who have met institutional standards for teaching graduate students as well as undergraduates.) In some cases, programs encourage or even require one of the committee members to come from outside the student's home department or university. Referred to as the "outside reader" or "external reviewer," this committee member may be chosen by the student or designated by the department.

The composition of a student's committee may change between its initial formation and the student's final thesis defense. Faculty members leave universities; they sometimes fall out with students or colleagues; sometimes they die. All such situations necessitate a replacement. In addition, students' research agendas sometimes shift, which might suggest that a committee member give way to someone with more appropriate expertise for the unfolding project. For the student, reconstituting a committee may be a delicate political matter that produces great anxiety.

What is a thesis proposal?

A thesis proposal, sometimes called a prospectus, is an agenda for research and writing. It usually outlines what problem will be investigated in a project, the methods of research the student will employ, the scholarly literature relevant to the project, and the significance of the study. Sometimes a proposal also includes a timetable for completion and a chapter outline. In some disciplines, the thesis proposal constitutes the first several chapters of the final thesis, usually the introduction, the literature review, and the methodological section (this approach presupposes a relatively quick process of data gathering and writing; otherwise the literature review would require updating to reflect scholarship published since the proposal defense). In other disciplines, the proposal is a single, more streamlined document that does not overlap with the finished thesis. In some programs in the sciences, a written dissertation proposal is not required; instead, students make an oral presentation to their committee members outlining their intended study. A dissertation proposal can be a useful foundation for writing fellowship and grant applications that require the graduate student to explain how he will spend his subsidized time.

In the course of preparing a dissertation proposal, students often realize that their intended projects are impossible or unwise. There can be a variety of possible reasons for this: primary sources may turn out not to exist; it may become clear that the intended experiments would take the remainder of the student's natural lifetime; the country in which the student intended to do fieldwork may become too dangerous to visit; someone else may have already conducted (or be in the midst of completing) an essentially identical project. In the event of such contingencies, a student who still wishes to forge ahead must brainstorm with his advisor a new route to a meaningful, manageable piece of original research.

Why does a student have to write a proposal before writing a thesis or dissertation?

It is tempting to want to skip this step of the dissertation process. If the student has in mind what he wants to do for his project and can communicate this orally to his thesis advisor, why not just go ahead and do it? The answer is that a Ph.D. dissertation, or even a master's thesis, is a complex undertaking that should be planned carefully before being executed. What would happen if the student completed a labor-intensive research process only to discover that someone else had already written about the results, that the experiments undertaken could not possibly lead to the anticipated result? What about the student who aspires to do a project best undertaken by a senior scholar? The proposal is an opportunity to get feedback from experienced researchers—the thesis committee—about whether the project is sound and significant. The few programs that omit a dissertation proposal are in the sciences, where students' research is part of a team effort coordinated by a lead principal investigator who needs to keep students graduating regularly.

A dissertation proposal is usually subject to an oral defense before it is approved. In a proposal hearing, the student's advisor and other committee members meet to talk about the plan. Depending on the committee's view of the student's work, the institutional culture, and their own temperaments, this meeting can be either exhilarating or unpleasant. Committee members might kindly offer helpful suggestions for improvement or endorse everything the student has written. On the other hand, they might critique the project fiercely or even send the student back to the drawing board to rethink the entire basis of the project.

Why do apparently good dissertation topics sometimes fall apart?

Even thoughtful dissertation topics may prove untenable. Sometimes a great idea proves to be untestable: the student cannot build the right equipment, perhaps; or it may be that there are not enough subjects to produce meaningful results. Another student might spend six months in an intellectual alley that leads to a dead end. There may be ethical or safety issues with a chosen topic: if the study involves human subjects, it has to be assessed by a review board. The IRB might reject the study because it presents a risk to participants. For reasons of both ethics and liability, for example, no university wants a graduate student to go out and give pregnant women LSD to find out how it affects their babies' cognitive development. At other times, the requirement that dissertation research be original presents a problem: midway through the research process, a graduate student might learn of someone else doing essentially the same project, but with a significant head start. Although the student may have

EXPERT TIP:

One way for a graduate student to avoid being scooped is to keep her ear to the ground at professional conferences. By listening to professional gossip and to paper sessions, it is possible to learn not only what people are saying about interesting topics, but who is working in emerging areas.

VOICE:

Students in law school do not spend three years and thousands of tuition dollars only to discover at the very end that diplomas are unattainable. Graduate students, like marathon runners, may have the finish line in sight and yet collapse.

— Steven M. Cahn, *Saints and Scamps*

the option of starting over or modifying the study at this point, she may be so discouraged at having wasted time that she abandons the project rather than try to complete the degree with unsatisfactory research results.

How long does it take to write a dissertation?

This varies by student and by discipline. In some disciplines, most of the work involved in completing a dissertation consists of doing research; in other fields, the time spent writing is as laborious as research. Dissertations are not like undergraduate papers; they cannot be successfully produced at the last minute. Even poor dissertations require at least several months of preparation. The authors of a guide to graduate school for women underscore the time commitment required: "Getting a graduate degree is a time-consuming, if not a time-devouring, experience."[2]

Mathematics graduate students spend a lot of time thinking and making notes about their problem. Many meet with their advisors regularly to report their findings, giving presentations (using a chalkboard or a computer) and discussing the ongoing challenges of their research. In the sciences, students conduct experiments that may take several years to come to fruition but require little writing time. Once such students have found the solution to their problem, however, actually writing up the dissertation might take only a few weeks and seem almost clerical, especially if they have already published most of their findings. Some routinely write articles about their research as they proceed and then simply revise their finished publications to meet their institution's formal requirements for a dissertation.

In the humanities and social sciences, however, writing up a dissertation is often at least as time-consuming as the research (which can itself take many months or even several years of burrowing into a library or archive or designing and implementing a survey or conducting a series of interviews). The reason it takes so long to write up this kind of dissertation is that only through the process of the writing itself do dissertators figure out their arguments. Instead of walking away from the research process knowing exactly what she needs to write, a student in these disciplines often figures out what her argument is by doing the writing, which for many people is a slow, painful process. Sometimes this process reveals research holes that send the writer back to the library or into the field to dig more. So writing the dissertation can take several years—several years after the student has completed all the coursework and passed the program's other hurdles.

In all disciplines, advisors and committees can require that students rewrite even a careful first draft. Some graduate students respond eagerly to critiques and revise their dissertations in short order. Others, unhappy with the criticism or their advisors, may take much longer to respond to a request for a rewrite, drawing out still further the process of filing a dissertation. Advisors can also cause delays: some are painfully slow to respond to drafts of chapters, meaning that a student cannot reasonably achieve anything else on that piece of the project until the feedback arrives.

Financial exigencies can also interfere with completing a dissertation. A graduate student in a program with a lot of funding might receive four or five years of support through fellowships, teaching and research assistantships, and grants. After that, even in generous programs, financial support from the home institution tends to taper off, and graduate students who are not yet finished must find ways to support themselves. Many ABD graduate students who hope to become professors find work as adjunct faculty, both to make money and to polish their professional credentials. Because adjunct jobs often pay poorly, graduate students may commit themselves to teaching several courses simultaneously, and teaching, while gratifying, can be a huge time drain for graduate students. Class preparation has a strict deadline, and meeting that near-term objective can override the need to write the dissertation, where the lead time is much longer. Other types of jobs, too, can distract graduate students from finishing: they take too much energy, require lengthy trips, or are intrinsically interesting. Graduate students may willingly throw themselves into doing any work they can find other than the dissertation, especially if suffering writer's block or experiencing psychological difficulty with research, writing, or an advisor.

May a graduate student seek professional writing services, such as those offered by ghostwriters or editors?

Writers who publish books and magazine or journal articles receive all kinds of professional help to improve their prose. Editors, copy editors, and sometimes ghostwriters shape what is published under an author's byline. The same range of options is not available to graduate students, who are seeking certification for their ability to do original research and express their new ideas in writing. Editors may be hired, but ghostwriters, whether paid or friendly free help, are strictly forbidden.

There are both ethical and practical problems with hiring a ghostwriter to write up a dissertation. The ethical problem is that graduate schools require dissertations to represent the student's own work; that is, the student is the author of the dissertation, with his or her name on it, and the thesis is what earns the degree. Part of the goal of producing a dissertation is to show that a student can do both the research and the writing required for the Ph.D. A graduate student who hires a ghostwriter to draft his thesis is no better than an undergraduate who buys a term paper off the Internet. A university that discovers a dissertation was ghostwritten will rescind a student's degree on grounds of academic misconduct.

The practical problem is that the research for a dissertation is supposed to be entirely original. This means that the only person who really understands the data well enough to write about it is the person who conducted the research; that is, the student. A ghostwriter would probably fabricate data as well as prose, thereby undermining the entire purpose of the graduate degree.

Hiring a copy editor is a different matter. Scholarship that is published in a journal or a book receives the attention of a professional expert who makes sure that the grammar is correct, the sentences make sense, and the text and illustrations look right. It is acceptable for a graduate student to hire a professional to copyedit a dissertation, especially if the advisor is unwilling or unable to do this task for the student (and many graduate advisors will not edit prose, rightly believing that their expertise is in the student's subject matter, not the production of polished writing). Hiring a copy editor can be especially valuable for a graduate student whose native language is not English. A student who has devoted her energy to her topic and not the intricacies of her word processor might also benefit from the help of someone who knows how to format everything according to university standards. Responsible editors, however, will not alter the substance of the student's ideas; they only make sure that the ideas are presented in a clean, professional manner.

What is a dissertation defense?

Most graduate schools require students who have completed their dissertations to defend them orally. A defense typically consists of the graduate student sitting down with members of his dissertation committee, which might include an "outside reader" (that is, a scholar from another department or institution), and talking about its strengths, weaknesses, and possibilities for revision for professional publication and future related projects. Some dissertation defenses are open to the public and advertised with flyers; others are confined to the dissertator and committee. In a few programs, there is no dissertation defense; the dissertation is finished when the committee members agree it is acceptable. Given these variables, the character of dissertation defenses varies widely. Some friendly dissertation committees offer only mild critiques and use the meeting to help the almost-Ph.D. think about the future. Others are hostile, and one or more members of the committee may fail the project (how many votes are needed to fail the dissertation varies from institution to institution).

Part of an advisor's responsibility is to prevent an unprepared student from defending. In some cases, a committee may require a student to make minor revisions to the thesis following the defense; at other institutions, changing the dissertation in any way following a successful defense is forbidden.

In most cases, the dissertation defense is the final hurdle in obtaining the doctorate. Once the dissertation is defended, the graduate student is no longer a student and may begin to use the title *Doctor*, even before the graduation ceremony.

Is a defended dissertation a finished dissertation?

After a student defends a dissertation, she must submit several copies to the university office that handles distribution. Typically, the degree-granting institution keeps one or two copies for its own library and sends one copy to UMI (University Microfilms), now owned by ProQuest. UMI preserves the dissertation and distributes it to subscribers and to people and libraries who pay for a copy (on microfilm or digitally). UMI issues royalties to the dissertation's author.

Because dissertations are, in this sense, published, they must conform to particular standards of appearance. In order to be microfilmed, for example, dissertations must have certain margins of white space around the edges of pages and be printed in a font large enough to remain legible when reproduced. The latter requirement may be obsolete in the digital age, but universities still want their students' scholarship to reflect well on them, so appearance continues to count. Universities employ people to make sure that dissertations comply with the required standards. The person who does this job, whether male or female, is often referred to as the Ruler Lady and regarded with fear, suspicion, or frustration. In point of fact, the Ruler Lady is often a friendly and helpful soul who understands that formatting problems crop up at the last minute. For the new graduate, after years of working on a dissertation, additional hours now spent making sure it is correctly formatted can be frustrating, especially if the Ruler Lady notices something that requires redesign of the entire document.

What happens to a dissertation after it is defended?

After a student files a polished and defended dissertation with the university, at a minimum the library will keep a copy to document the intellectual life of the institution. Cataloging the thesis means that bibliographic search engines, like WorldCat, will harvest the information about its existence so that other scholars can discover it. The submission of a copy of the dissertation to ProQuest's UMI enables people curious about the dissertation's contents to order a copy for their personal libraries.

The future of the successfully defended dissertation is largely up to the new graduate. Some students persevere up to graduation, collapse at the finish line, and then want nothing more to do with the project. Others have already published its major findings as articles and move on to new intellectual pastures. Many dissertation defenses, however, center on the question of what the new graduate needs to do to revise and prepare the work for publication either in scholarly journals or as a book. Some graduates take a few months or a year away from the work and then revisit it with fresh eyes and motivation, wishing to share the product of their labor with a broader audience. Because the point of scholarship is to disseminate new ideas, graduates should try to share their ideas broadly by publishing them.

CHAPTER 6

The Academic Culture

When I entered my doctoral program, I assumed, too readily as it turned out, that I should call all my professors by their first names. My advisor, one of the most easygoing, genial human beings one could hope to meet, signed all the notes and e-mails he sent undergraduate and graduate students alike with his name, Henry (although, as he aged, he noticed that students increasingly could bring themselves to address him only as Professor Binford). Taking my cue from him, I addressed all of the faculty members with a similar level of informality. This backfired on me, however, when one of them was annoyed when the undergraduates in my discussion section referred to her by her first name on her midterm course evaluations. She chastised me for encouraging football players, among others, to think of her so intimately and informally.

Navigating the mores of academic culture is tricky business. The rules are rarely put in writing, and they vary from person to person. New academics need to pay close attention to discover the boundaries within which they and their peers operate. The good news is that the intensive character of graduate education creates plenty of opportunities to observe the culture. This chapter provides some shortcuts to figuring out what the rules—and questions—are.

What do the terms *assistant professor* and *associate professor* mean?

The labels most often used to differentiate among the people who teach in colleges and universities are variations on *professor, lecturer,* or *instructor*. Generally the teachers of graduate students are members of a university's permanent faculty; that is, the people who teach graduate students hold appointments as professors.

Professors normally come in three ranks: assistant, associate, and full. Assistant professors are beginners; they have fewer years of experience and lack tenure. Typically, after six years an assistant professor can apply for tenure and promotion to associate professor. At some institutions, promotion and tenure are separate processes. When associate professors have accumulated more publications and experience, they can be promoted to full professor. It is not usual to address someone as Associate Professor Smith or Assistant Professor Jones. The terms are ranks, not titles.

In addition, some institutions grant extraordinary rank to some faculty members. These scholars may be ranked as distinguished professor, university professor, or emeritus/a professor. Distinguished and university professors are full professors whose achievements are so outstanding that they deserve special accolades. Such ranks are not a normal part of the promotion ladder; faculty usually aspire to be promoted to full professors as part of their career path, but only a select few hope to attain the more exalted laurels. When a professor retires, she can request recognition from her institution as emerita (Latin for "earned by service"; a male professor requests to become emeritus). Professors may retire without requesting this distinction. At my institution, emeriti faculty give up their offices but gain free campus parking.

Although assistant professors, who usually have recently completed dissertations, tend to be on the cutting edge of their fields, some universities and departments discourage or forbid assistant professors from heading dissertation committees. The reasons for this practice vary. Sometimes the institution is trying to protect its junior faculty members from being overburdened with time-consuming responsibilities during their probationary period. In other cases, the institution intends for the tenure-track period to be a time of training, so assistant professors may sit on thesis committees in order to learn the ropes and provide their expertise. In some programs in the sciences, however, assistant professors must supervise a certain number of theses before they are eligible for promotion. A graduate student whose advisor is an assistant professor runs the risk of having his advisor fired midway through the student's research projects.

What is tenure?

Tenure is the right of a professor to hold her job for life, without running the risk of being fired. In theory, tenure protects academic freedom: the right of a faculty member to pursue her scholarly convictions in research or teaching and to speak out publicly without having to worry that unpopular or controversial ideas will result in her removal. Following the recommendations of the American Association of University Professors, most (though not all) colleges and universities in the United States offer their faculty (and sometimes their librarians) some form of tenure.

In general, there are two ways to achieve tenure. One is to serve in a "tenure track" professorship and then apply for tenure; the other is to be hired with tenure after service elsewhere. The usual probationary period is seven years; in the normal course of events, an applicant applies for tenure during his sixth year, and his tenure begins with the seventh year. Someone who is denied tenure is, following the rejection, usually granted a terminal year in which to find new employment. This may seem like a generous amount of time for a job search, but a faculty member who does not find a new academic job during that year may never secure another tenure-track position. The criteria for granting tenure vary from institution to institution and are sometimes spelled out and sometimes clouded in fog. A very few of the most elite institutions, like Harvard University, generally expect not to tenure any of their assistant professors but instead draw their tenured faculty only from professors who have proven their worth at other schools. At universities that grant doctorates, to qualify for tenure faculty are usually expected to maintain an active research and publication program in addition to regular teaching. At schools that do not offer advanced degrees, tenure criteria tend to relate more to quality of teaching and institutional service than to quantity and significance of published scholarship.

Graduate students need to have a basic grasp of the concept of tenure to understand whom on their program faculty to cultivate as advisors. An assistant professor who appears unlikely to fulfill the tenure requirements is not a good candidate for a dissertation advisor because he will probably not be around to see the doctoral

VOICE:

Who wouldn't want the ultimate in job security? As a professor, if you fulfill minimal performance requirements (e.g., teaching a class every semester) and maintain at least minimal moral standards (love affairs with your students are sometimes frowned upon), and if your university doesn't shut down your department entirely in response to severe economic stress, you have a guaranteed paycheck. In fact, universities have long since recognized the economic significance of tenure. University salaries would certainly have to be higher if professors were subject to being laid off.

—Peter J. Feibelman, *A Ph.D. Is Not Enough*

student through to completion of her degree. The reverse of this problem might come up in the case of an assistant professor who is so brilliant and productive that she is likely to be scouted by another institution. She might or might not be able to take her graduate students with her to her new job. Because tenured faculty are much less mobile, they make more stable dissertation advisors and committee members. Master's students need to worry less about these distinctions because their timetables are shorter.

How should graduate students address professors?

How graduate students (and students in general) should address professors is a question that combines etiquette and personal taste. Faculty in professional and arts programs may hold a terminal master's degree or even no degree beyond the bachelor's, but most graduate faculty in the liberal arts hold a Ph.D. When addressing a Ph.D., either Doctor or Professor is generally acceptable, but because doctorates are so common among faculty members and are in fact a basic entrance requirement in the profession, some faculty disdain the doctor title. While merited, the use of Doctor can be seen as pretentious because in America's ostensibly classless, democratic society, only people in professions where instant obedience is vital, such as medicine or the military, really need hierarchical courtesy titles. On the other hand, for someone concerned to broadcast his status, Doctor can be seen as less respectful than Professor, because there are fewer professors than Ph.Ds.

Undergraduate students may find it not always appropriate to use the Professor form of address because many people teaching college classes are adjunct faculty. There is, however, some debate on this point: many people insist that anyone who teaches at college level is entitled to be called a professor. But only in exceedingly rare cases are graduate students taught by instructors who are not also appointed to their jobs with the rank of assistant, associate, or plain-vanilla professor.

At some institutions, the cultural norm is to address all instructors as Mr. or Ms., regardless of the teacher's degree or rank. This tendency appears especially at older, elite, private schools such as Bryn Mawr College and the University of Chicago.

Female members of the academy rarely change their names if they marry (which they do at a lower rate than other women in American culture), so Ms. is almost always a safer bet than Mrs. There are, however, a few women with Ph.D.s who use their husband's names and prefer to be addressed as Mrs. Moreover, some women faculty, especially those who are young and untenured, are sensitive about the use of Ms. When they hear students refer to male faculty as Professor or Doctor and women as Ms., they may suspect that the students do not respect the authority of women. Faculty members of any gender who are proud of their accomplishments may insist that they have earned the right to a courtesy title.

Some faculty members are perfectly comfortable with graduate students calling them by their first names. Participation in the free-wheeling culture of the 1960s and 1970s, in which many of today's faculty (now of retirement-age) came of age, took particular glee in transgressing the customs of formal society such as the use of titles and other signifiers of structural inequalities; democratizing the classroom and calling authority into question were integral parts of their pedagogy. One legacy of their subversion of authority is the standing question of whether graduate students are really junior colleagues or senior pupils. If the former, then reciprocal use of first names recognizes that teacher and student are engaged in the same basic project (academic inquiry), even if they are temporarily at different stages of the process. On the other hand, some faculty members insist that graduate students still engaged in coursework use a formal title with them; but then, upon completion of some hurdle (such as preliminary exams or the dissertation proposal), they invite a student to use the professor's first name, welcoming the maturing student as a newly minted peer.

These already complex considerations are further complicated by the feelings of the graduate student. Faculty members, as the superior partner in what is structurally a power relationship, are the ones who have the implicit right to set the terms of the interactions. Nonetheless, a student from a formal culture might feel uneasy calling a professor by her first name. A student with her analytic gaze cast toward hierarchy might have political reasons for preferring to call her professor by his first name (thereby disrupting the power dynamic) or, on the other hand, to address him only formally (thereby underlining and perhaps drawing attention to their status differential). A student whose parents are informally inclined academics might regard as stuffy and arrogant a professor who insists on being called Doctor. Because faculty members usually have some sort of power over the student (in the form of ability to give grades or write letters of recommendation), a wise graduate student will usually stifle his own feelings on the matter and let the faculty member in question be the guide.

Some professors are aware of the dilemma faced by students who do not know what their advisors prefer and sign notes and e-mails with their preferred designation. Others appear oblivious to the fact that their advisees of many years have never addressed them by any name or title and begin all written and verbal interactions with a simple, "Hello, there" or even "Hey." Some of my own graduate students, who place great stock on the significance of the doctorates they seek, have compromised with my preference for informality by calling me Doctor Amanda. Absent a sensitive hint or a clear institutional culture, the best way to find out how to address a professor is to ask.

EXPERT TIP:
How can a graduate student find out what a professor prefers to be called? Certainly, graduate students can find out the scuttlebutt by asking classmates or other faculty members. But the direct approach should not hurt: "Excuse me, professor X, what do you prefer for me to call you?" Professors—who make scholarly inquiry their business—will generally not be offended by such a direct and polite question.

What role does institutional prestige play in a graduate student's personal reputation?

The hierarchy of American colleges, topped by elite, private, wealthy institutions, is widely recognized. The rankings of the hierarchy, however, matter more to undergraduates and faculty than to graduate students. For graduate students, the *program* matters more than the *institution* that grants the degree.

Graduate degrees are supposed to signify advanced training in research, although in practice some programs are more rigorous than others. Nettles and Millett point out that "the graduate is a grand and desirable package, but the enclosed goods may be highly variable."[1] Ph.D. program excellence is usually judged by the quality of the faculty, and even though the general undergraduate program of a university might not be held in particularly high regard, that institution may have carefully cultivated a few top-notch Ph.D. programs. Conversely, the best undergraduate institutions can have weak advanced-degree programs.

Admision to a Ph.D. program depends not only on a student's grades but also on the quality of the program she previously attended (the latter being the case when the applicant already holds a master's degree), but having gone to the "best" program does not guarantee the kind of job the Ph.D. recipient yearns for. For example, selective liberal arts colleges sometimes are suspicious of applicants for professorial positions who have never attended a small college; the search committee may wonder whether a person with lots of fellowship support and little classroom experience is serious about a career devoted to teaching. A good way for a student to decide which graduate program to attend is to choose a department he would like to join one day and then look at the research and educational histories of faculty who teach there.

While program prestige might suggest that a graduate student's work is of high quality, students cannot rely on this factor bolstering their future careers. Advisors' reputations may help, but they do not define the student. Academics know that a weak student may slide through a strong program and that a weak program can produce a great student. Career achievement ultimately depends on the individual student more than on his pedigree.

How do scholars disseminate their research findings at conferences?

Academics share ideas and get feedback from interested colleagues from other institutions by presenting their in-progress work at conferences with a paper or poster. At a typical conference, several people present papers orally in a panel format and then hear comments and questions, both from a senior colleague who has read the papers in advance and from members of the audience. For projects with multiple authors, being designated as the presenter for the group is a sign of being central to the project.

Conference sessions are generally organized through a program committee. Scholars wanting to present papers send an abstract or a completed paper to the program committee, which decides which papers to accept. Selection is based on the papers' quality, relationship to the conference theme, the possibility of organizing similar papers into a substantively related panel, and the size of the conference venue. Sometimes the presenters organize themselves into groups ahead of time, recruiting other presenters, a session chair, and the discussant, and submitting the panel as a whole for acceptance or rejection.

In some disciplines, presenters may offer a conference poster instead of a conference paper. Instead of showing up in a hotel room at a designated time to read their papers to an audience, presenters display their findings on posters that other people walk by and read at their convenience during the conference, chatting with the poster presenter.

Why is it important to present work in progress at conferences?

Faculty members encourage graduate students to give conference papers for several reasons: it enables them to meet other people interested in their work; it brings them fresh feedback and ideas from scholars unfamiliar with their work; they themselves become known; and it builds the student's CV.

Conferences are a major way in which academics from different institutions get to know each other. Connections made with colleagues can yield multiple benefits for the presenter: valuable feedback on the work itself, the opportunity to collaborate on future projects, invitations to deliver colloquium presentations, letters of recommendation, and even postdoctoral and tenure-track job opportunities all can flow from conference networking.

Sometimes a presentation can lead to publication—the coin of the realm in academia. A journal or book series editor (usually a professor) or an acquisitions editor from an academic press (usually a publishing professional) might approach the author of an interesting paper and invite him to submit his work, when it is ready, for publication.

Why do presenters have to pay to attend a conference?

It is very possible for a graduate student, especially one who is cash-strapped, to think about presenting a conference paper in terms something like this: "When I share my (wonderful and exciting) new ideas at a conference, I am doing the conference a favor. I have paid to travel to the conference venue and stay in a hotel that is beyond my normal budget. Not only should I not have to pay to attend the conference, but they should pay me."

However, realistically there are many other considerations to bear in mind. Putting on a conference costs the sponsoring organization money. The space for the conference must be reserved and rented more than a year in advance. Any included refreshments and meals must be paid for. Organizing, designing, printing, and distributing the conference program are expensive activities. Conference papers do benefit the conference, but they also benefit the presenter, who gets valuable feedback, networking opportunities, a line on his CV, and a working vacation. So everyone who participates in a conference should help to pay for it. Sometimes conference organizers, aware of how difficult it can be for graduate students to pay for conferences, offer reduced registration rates to encourage their participation.

Sometimes universities maintain a pool of funds to defray the costs of their graduate students who present papers at conferences, and grant recipients build conference travel into their budgets. A graduate student who spends a significant portion of personal income to travel to a conference without reimbursement should consult with a tax advisor about whether the costs can be deducted from income taxes.

What is peer review?

Peer review distinguishes academic publishing from commercial publishing. In peer review, someone in the field other than the author reads and comments on the quality and significance of a work submitted for publication before it is put into print. Peer review also provides a check against fraud—plagiarism and the fabrication of data—by people intimately familiar with the field. Both journal publishers and university presses build peer review into their editorial practices. Granting agencies, such as those sponsored by the federal government, also use a peer review process to help determine who should receive their funds. Peer reviewers may say that the submitted work is terrific and should be published essentially as it is; or they may say it should be revised slightly, or that it should be revised thoroughly and resubmitted for consideration; or they may reject it altogether.

Generally, the author of a book or article does not know who the reviewer is. The process is called peer review even when the author is a lowly graduate student and the reviewer is a senior person in the field. The governing idea is that it is the scholarship itself, not the author, that is up for judgment.

Academic journals usually use "double-blind peer review" for articles. This means that the author's name is stripped from the article before it is sent out for consideration, and neither the reviewers nor the authors know each other's identities. University presses tend to use a single-blind process of peer review for books. The reviewers know who the author is, but the author does not know who the reviewers are. Especially in the humanities, which are book-driven disciplines, by the time a scholar is ready to publish his research as a book, he has usually presented portions of it at conferences and published interesting bits as journal articles. Trying to protect the author's identity in such a case would be pointless.

That, in theory, is how peer review works. In practice, some fields are small enough that the reviewers and the authors all know each other's identities. Whether they later identify themselves to each other hinges on politics and personality.

How can a graduate student find out which journals are worth reading regularly?

Graduate students are routinely advised to read regularly the important journals in their fields and, when they are able, to submit their scholarship for publication. Some journals are famous and it is obvious that they are at the top of the heap: even people outside of the sciences know that breakthrough advances are published (and publicized) in *Science* and *Nature* and that the latest and most important general medical scholarship appears in the *New England Journal of Medicine* and the *Lancet*. For the most part, however, journals are less-well-known and students are expected to intuit the names of the most important ones in their field.

There are at least three ways to figure this out. First, in most disciplines the major professional organizations also publish a journal that covers the sweep of the field. Members join the organization and the journal is sent to them automatically. Articles published in these journals are not necessarily directly relevant to a student's particular research interests, but they give an important indication of the intellectual landscape of the field.

Second, graduate students notice the sources of the articles they are assigned to read in classes. Most professors want their students to read scholarship that is important rather than work that is insignificant, and authors of important work usually avoid publishing it someplace obscure. When researching the existing literature, students notice which journal titles come up frequently.

Third, they ask. Early on in their years of school or when switching to new areas of research, academics get a free pass on asking questions that appear to be hopelessly ignorant. As long as a student is still starting out learning new areas, there is no harm in asking "What journals should I be reading to get to know this field?"

What counts as an important journal?

Academics, like other humans, think that prestige and popularity matter. While publishing their scholarship anywhere is good, publishing it in a widely read or prestigious journal is better. So how do academics know which journals they should aspire to publish in? This, too, can be researched.

One measure of a journal's prestige is its rejection rate. A high rejection rate suggests to readers that lots of people want to have their work included in the journal but only a few make the cut. Another measure of prestige is found in the journal's "citation index." This measure counts how many scholars have cited a given book or article. University libraries routinely carry books (and, increasingly, electronic databases) that publish the rejection rate and citation indices for academic journals. In quantitatively oriented fields, researchers are expected to report not only their publications on their annual reviews and promotion cases, but also to list the journals' rejection rate and how often their articles have been cited.

Who did the most work for a book or journal article that has more than one author?

Because it is through publication that research scholars measure their worth, everyone wants to know who is responsible for a given piece of writing. In most humanities fields, most works are by a single author, but in other disciplines, collaborative work is standard, and readers want to know who is responsible for what and to what degree. Everyone who contributed to the research for a project gets credit by having their name included in the byline of the article, even if the main ideas originated with just one or some of those listed. For some highly coordinated projects in which the work takes place in multiple laboratories, the list of authors can run into the dozens—or hundreds, leading to concerns about "authorship inflation." In fields where collaborative work is the norm, doctoral students routinely graduate with several articles to their credit, and scholars who have been working for decades may have hundreds of publications.

It is tempting to assume that the person whose name is first on the list of authors did the most for the project. But is that "most important person" the one who had the original idea, the one who performed the key experiments, the one wrote up the results, or the one headed the lab? All of those are important responsibilities, but different fields allocate the credit for the important work differently. In many cases, the first author listed is understood to be the lead author. Sometimes the last person listed is understood to be the main author. Sometimes names are listed alphabetically or, for frequent collaborators, in a rotating list. Sometimes the owner of the lab, the "principal investigator," is listed first, even if all he did was sign off on a finished article researched and written by someone else.

Recently, authors of articles in *Nature* petitioned for the inclusion of footnotes on author lists, indicating that two or more authors contributed equally and therefore deserved full credit for being lead authors.[2] In most disciplines, some standard convention determines authorship order. The e-mail address of an article's "corresponding author" is a good clue about who coordinated a project.

At least once, whimsy decided authorship credit. In the 1940s, graduate student Ralph Alpher wrote a paper about the amount of certain elemental matter in the early universe, under the supervision of his advisor, George Gamow. Wishing to play on the assonance of their names with the first three letters of the Greek alphabet, α, β, and Γ, Gamow added the name of his colleague Hans Bethe to the article, submitting it under the authorship of "Alpher, Bethe, and Gamow." Alpher was not amused by a move that threatened his credit for a major scholarly breakthrough, but he was stuck with publication in that format.[3]

Understanding the rules for authorship order is a vital skill for novice scholars. Scientists who do not receive field-appropriate credit for the work they conducted risk their professional futures.

How do scholarly journals compensate their authors?

Having a scholarly article accepted for publication is a real coup for a graduate student. A peer-reviewed publication helps the student gain recognition in the discipline, circulates her ideas, and builds her CV. Increasingly, faculty search committees weed out candidates who do not have publications in their portfolios. But in many ways, scholarly publishing is not like commercial publishing, and where a freelance journalist would not agree to publish an article (or even accept a writing assignment!) without a fee, academic authors write primarily for the glory. My contract for this book was accompanied by a handout from the press, cautioning, "With rare exceptions, the greater 'profit' to the author comes not from royalties earned, but from professional advancement resulting from publication."[4]

The lack of reimbursement for writing journal articles is rooted in the economics of journal production. Much of the staffing is volunteer: the editors receive little, if any, compensation for their work; nor do the scholars who peer review (although a graduate student working as a research assistant for a scholarly journal does receive a stipend). The major expense of producing such journals lies in printing and distributing them to libraries, which purchase most of the subscriptions. Scholarly journals themselves are often nonprofit (although some are commercial and charge for subscriptions); their revenue comes from a modest amount of paid advertising and from subscriptions (which vary from around $30 annually in some humanities fields to thousands of dollars in some science disciplines). They simply do not have the money to pay authors. In effect, universities act as the patrons of research scholars, paying them salaries that enable them to devote their time to producing publishable scholarship that is not otherwise paid. Graduate students, of course, write articles without the financial salary cushion afforded faculty.

Why does a scholarly author sometimes have to pay to have his work considered or published by a journal?

In many fields, scholars do not pay to have their work peer reviewed. Journals exist for the same reason as research scholars and universities: to cultivate and disseminate new ideas as widely as possible. But in a few, practically oriented disciplines, some of the more prestigious, high-circulating, and high-impact journals gener-

ate revenue from authors. Sometimes the journal editors have decided to defray the cost of subscriptions by charging authors. In
some cases, authors submitting work for consideration by an editor
and peer reviewer pay for the privilege of receiving evaluations; in
other cases, only authors whose work is accepted are required to
pay "page fees." Scientists incorporate page fees into their grant
applications, so graduate students in those disciplines do not pay
out of pocket to have their research published. But even in the cases
where journals do not charge their writers, authors may be personally responsible for the cost of reproducing copyrighted images or
words covered under permissions regulations.

Should graduate students try to publish their research before their dissertations are finished?

Any graduate student who aspires to a job with a significant research
component, whether as a professor, in government, or industry,
should try to publish her research before she graduates. Publishing
is so standard in the sciences that it amounts to a requirement of the
course of study. From the start of their graduate programs, doctoral
students work in labs productive enough to be grant-funded, so
getting coauthor credit is almost automatic. But graduate students
in the sciences also need primary-author credits for one or more
articles in order to show that they are capable of conceptualizing
their own programs of scholarly research.

Publication of peer-reviewed articles by students in the humanities and social sciences was fairly unusual but not unheard of
when I went to graduate school in the early 1990s. Competition for
professorial positions has intensified so much since then that most
successful finalists for research-oriented positions have at least one
or two published or forthcoming articles on their CVs. It may be
easier for graduate students to garner publication credits such as
book reviews or encyclopedia entries by soliciting editors of appropriate journals and projects, but in the absence of peer-reviewed
articles, this sort of "service" publication carries little weight on the

research job market. Applicants for positions at teaching-oriented liberal arts and community colleges need to devote much more of their extracurricular energies to improving their pedagogical skills, but rarely does a peer-reviewed article hurt their chances.

How much publication is enough?

With the American academic job market in a perpetual state of ever-worsening crisis since the 1970s, the professionalization of graduate students has ratcheted up in lockstep, with increasing publication expectations for candidates for assistant professor positions. A recent study of doctoral education in the United States found that "research productivity," that is, presenting scholarship at conference or publishing above and beyond the requirements of the dissertation, is positively correlated with completion of the doctorate in all fields.[5] Some graduate students strategically delay finishing their dissertations so that they can get a couple of articles into the pipeline before they defend and go on the job market. They calculate that an extra year of voluntary poverty is worth a better shot at a permanent position. Another tactic is to take a basic dataset and parcel it out into separate articles, each one molded into the "least publishable unit," that is, a single independent and novel but relatively unimportant idea.

At a certain point, however, quality of scholarship must outweigh quantity. Academic search committees do notice when graduate students have been enrolled for an excessively long stretch of time without other gainful employment, and they do read the publications that applicants submit as part of the evidence of their suitability for the position. While a list of publications might get an applicant noticed, a single article that is significant enough to shake up a field should outweigh a long list of minor "pubs."

How do graduate students celebrate the completion of their degrees?

Earning an advanced degree requires so much time and dedication that graduate students are often exhausted and relieved at the end of the process. One new doctorate fell asleep at the dinner party celebrating her achievement. Some attend graduation jubilantly; others want nothing more to do with the institution. I did not attend my own doctoral graduation in part because almost an entire year had elapsed between my dissertation defense and my ceremony. But I also felt that my rewards included my personal satisfaction and my good fortune in obtaining a tenure-track job, so why did I need an event? Other graduate students recognize the importance of acknowledging milestones in their lives, enjoy a good party, or at least dinner and a celebratory bottle of champagne.

Graduate students might also enjoy a graduation gift, a self-funded splurge, or a spree funded by a loving relative. Appropriate gifts for graduate students may include a special fountain pen, a new computer, money to pay off student loans, a vacation, or the cost of the hood and gown that has to be rented for the graduation ceremony.

A framed diploma, however, might not be an appropriate present. In some professions, visible establishment of credentials, especially in the form of diplomas hanging on the office wall, is the norm. Therapists, doctors, and accountants reassure their clients and patients that they are credentialed authorities by displaying their degrees and certifications. Such displays are considered ostentatious in the academy. In theory, everyone who merits his own college office has a doctorate, so why brag? People with Ph.D.s who work in colleges and universities might hang their diplomas in their homes, but almost never at work. Someone with a Ph.D. who works outside of the academy, however, might well want to remind the people he works with that he warrants being called Doctor.

Is a Ph.D. the only kind of doctorate?

No. In the same way that there are many different kinds of master's degrees, there are many different kinds of doctorates. It is possible to earn non-Ph.D. doctorates in education, divinity, and public health, to name just a few. There are good, professional reasons for people to pursue these doctorates. In general, however, the Ph.D. is regarded as the premier *research* doctorate and is a prerequisite for most professorial jobs.

CHAPTER 7

Having a Life in Graduate School

One of my friends in graduate school did something so awful she did not want anyone to know: she got pregnant. It was not that she was unmarried that made her pregnancy deviant; it was that she was a graduate student. Shortly after the baby started to show, her advisor walked by her desk in the library and stopped to chat. My friend related the story of sinking lower and lower in her chair, hiding her swollen belly under the surface of her desk and wishing her advisor would stop talking and go away. Eventually, of course, she could not hide her condition any longer. But many faculty assume that graduate students put their lives on hold while they study, and she could not anticipate what kind of reception her pregnancy would get.

Not every woman who goes to graduate school is fortunate enough to be the student of Harvard historian Laurel Thatcher Ulrich, who is reputed to make her pregnant students quilts as celebratory gifts. Or to attend Berkeley or Princeton Universities, which have instituted paid maternity leave for graduate students. Even as late as the mid-1990s, my friend felt that by getting pregnant while studying for a doctorate, she ran a risk of being seen as less than serious about completing her degree. Most graduate students who are audacious enough to have babies while still in school expect little in the way of sympathy or accommodations from their departments and institutions.

Having a baby is only one aspect of having a life. While graduate students are in school, they remain people, and sometimes people have priorities in life other than their studies. This chapter will address questions about how people in graduate school continue to live their lives, even while retaining their educational goals.

Why do prospective graduate students often relocate to attend school?

Many people who pursue Ph.D.s aspire to jobs as professors after graduation. The best initial strategy a potential professor can employ toward attaining this goal is to go to the best graduate program (with a good fit for her specific interests) that admits and funds her generously. Higher-ranked graduate programs tend to have faculty who are better-known and respected in their fields, more funding opportunities, better libraries, and a better track record of placing recent graduates in tenure-track jobs. These factors explain their high ranking. Simply put, if it means leaving home to attend graduate school, doing so is often a wise move for a student's long-term career.

Many good, but not top-tier, public universities offer interesting graduate programs that might have some appeal. Indeed, students do relocate from other places to attend them. Here the matter of intellectual fit becomes crucial. Even university departments with relatively large faculties can only rarely sustain complete coverage of their fields. Instead of trying to be everything to all comers, departments tend to specialize. This is especially true in the sciences, where scholars benefit from pooling their research expertise in labs and joint publications. All chemistry faculty, for example, know enough to teach a foundation sequence of chemistry courses to undergraduates. But a given chemistry department's research expertise might focus on three or four distinct areas of the field, leaving others entirely uncovered. University faculty can advise graduate students within their areas of expertise but are foolish to try to do so beyond their basic competence. So, a potential graduate student whose interests diverge wildly from the basic research interests on the faculty of the local public university are unlikely to be well served by pursuing a Ph.D. there.

But for some students, relocation is simply impossible. Graduate students whose partners have careers that cannot be moved, who are bound to a particular region because of a divorce agreement, who are caring for aging parents, who have minor children who need to stay in their present schools, or whose source of income is a job that they will not relinquish while they pursue their advanced degrees often cannot go to the program that would otherwise be best for them. Such students, further, may also be unwilling to relocate anywhere in the country that they can find a tenure-track job upon completion of their degree. There certainly are valid reasons for someone who does not want to be a professor to obtain a Ph.D., but being unable to leave home for graduate school does not bode well for that person's long-run chances of maintaining an academic career.

None of that is to say, however, that a student who attends an ill-respected, local public university cannot produce first-rate scholarship or win the coveted tenure-track position; only that it is easier to develop an academic career when starting from a higher point.

What kinds of extracurricular activities should graduate students participate in?

High school students and undergraduate students are often advised to engage in extracurricular activities in order to show their future colleges and employers that they are well-rounded candidates. This advice does not apply to a graduate student whose sole aim is to become a professor: no search committee is going to care about your gourmet cooking or your stint volunteering with the homeless if your research and teaching are not up to snuff. Academic hiring committees are not looking for generalists; they want specialists. Graduate students who are focused on the professoriate should expend their energies researching the best dissertation and teaching the most dynamic courses they are capable of.

However, graduate students who are thinking of nonacademic career options—which in the twenty-first century ought to include almost all graduate students in the humanities, given the tightness of the academic job market—should continue to participate in hobbies that engage their interests and develop their talents. The authors of the standard advice manual for "postacademic" careers suggest that everyone needs a plan B. They point out that the skills cultivated in extracurricular work not only nourish graduate students psychologically but also illustrate how their skills can be deployed productively outside the academy. When they apply for nonacademic jobs, students who have maintained outside interests will have a track record.[1]

What do nonacademics understand about graduate students?

One of the biggest laments among graduate students is the difficulty of explaining themselves to nonacademics. Graduate students have immersed themselves in a strange new world of knowledge and a culture whose norms and expectations are unfamiliar to many of the people who love them. Well-meaning relations and friends are notorious for asking questions, making comments, and offering suggestions that graduate students interpret as criticism and pressure. Perhaps the most notorious of these questions is, "Why aren't you finished yet?" Of course, such questioners have no intention of sending the graduate student over the edge; they genuinely want to understand what he or she is going through and what they can do to help.

Even if graduate students feel that the subject of their studies is too complex to explain to outsiders, they can try to explain academic life more generally. A host of advice books about graduate school are available through university and public libraries. Some of the more useful and amusing of them are described in the section

"For Further Reading." Sharing one of these books with someone curious about graduate school can help explain the ins and outs of academic life while deflecting concerns about one's own progress.

Prospective nonacademic employers may be ambivalent about a job seeker's advanced education, suspecting that the candidate cares only about research, lacks practical skills, and cannot work in a team. Books such as Jerald Jellison's *Life after Grad School* suggest how graduate students can interpret their skills on the non-academic job market.[2]

Can dropping out of graduate school be a good decision?

The single best thing I ever did as a professor was to give a student permission to drop out. Although a student who chooses not to complete a graduate degree might feel like a failure, the decision to leave a graduate program without a diploma often makes sense. If nothing else, graduate school tends to promote self-reflection.

Along the way to the degree, a student may realize that she actually hates what she is studying; that he does not want to be a professor; that she does not have the necessary skills or imagination to win that dreamed-of Nobel prize; that his studies interfere with other personal priorities; or that he or she is simply better equipped to do something else. Deciding to go to graduate school is often a good decision; deciding to quit almost always is as well.

Why do graduate students sometimes avoid family gatherings?

Graduate school can shift, even skew, a student's priorities. Graduate students make all sorts of personal decisions that seem bizarre, even inexplicable, to their friends and families. Sometimes they even skip family events that other people view as command performances.

The specific reason for a graduate student's refusal to participate in family activities depends, of course, on the particular student and his circumstances. He may have an incomplete that he needs to clear before the next semester starts. She may plead the necessity of devoting a stretch of time to writing the dissertation between semesters because she is otherwise too busy teaching classes. He may be butting up against the university's time limits. She may not be able to face that wedding or Thanksgiving dinner where Uncle Bob is going to ask—again—when she is going to finish that everlasting degree.

The more general reason for such antisocial behavior is that successful graduate study requires a certain self-centered concentration. To achieve their goals, graduate students often put themselves and their needs first, for at least a portion of their lives. That self-centered time may come daily or sporadically, but for many students it feels necessary.

How much work do graduate students have to do between semesters?

Formal coursework represents only a limited portion of graduate students' work. In structuring classes, professors typically assign a discrete amount of reading and writing that can be accomplished within the time frame of the semester. But to get a good handle on their fields—that is, to know enough to merit the master's or doctoral degree—students need to become directors of their own work. A good portion of this task is figuring out what scholarship to read, beyond formal assignments. Much of this material, essential to the thesis or dissertation, is never suggested by a professor but emerges from the research process. Students working in labs continue their research without regard for the academic calendar. The end of classes means more time for research, not a break.

So for many graduate students, their choice to read and not play seems inconvenient or rude to friends and family who expect them to take a break, maybe even to go on vacation.

What are the difficulties of maintaining a romantic relationship during graduate school?

Many aspects of graduate study turn people inward, especially into their heads instead of their hearts. Graduate school demands many hours of students' time, sending them off to the lab, the library, or the field to do research for hours and even months, leaving them

VOICE:

Research—knowledge creation—is full of disappointments and failures. Hence, these years are not likely to be emotionally comfortable, well-balanced, or easygoing ones. In order to come through such a stressful experience unscathed, it is extremely important that you possess an inner certitude that you have made the right choices, that you are pursuing your true calling. It must be practically the only thing you want to do in life because, for a while at least, it will become almost synonymous with your life. As a consequence, it will also increase the pressure on personal relationships and generate a feedback effect on your academic performance. In short, many sacrifices will need to be made for a successful entry into the profession.

—John Komlos in *The Chicago Guide to Your Academic Career*

with little energy or opportunity to maintain an intimate relationship. Both the internal focus and the intensity of graduate study can undermine a student's ability to devote herself to her romantic partner. These difficulties can be exacerbated when the partner is unfamiliar with or unsympathetic to how graduate study affects the student. In graduate school, as in other areas of life, some wonderful, and some terrible, relationships are formed and broken.

Why are sexual relations between students and faculty forbidden?

At many institutions in the United States, professors are simply forbidden to date or have sex with their students. Even tenured professors risk a variety of sanctions if a complaint of sexual impropriety against them is borne out. The reasons rest in the inherent imbalance of power between faculty members and students. To a large extent, faculty members have power over the future of the lives of students: they assign grades, write letters of recommendation for jobs, and network on behalf of their students; if they fail to do these things, they can undermine a student's professional future. While undergraduates often are under a professor's authority only once over the course of their careers as students, graduate students' relationships with faculty normally extend over many years. Although faculty and graduate students often work as colleagues, the power imbalance conditions their relationship. Insofar as graduate students work as teachers, they, too, are enjoined from dating their students.

From the graduate student perspective, there are additional reasons to avoid personal entanglements with faculty. A graduate student who is happily dating a professor risks the opprobrium of peers, who may suspect that the student is receiving undue professional favors (letters of recommendation, high grades, coveted job opportunities) because of the relationship. In another kind of scenario, a graduate student whose relationship with a professor turns sour risks various repercussions, such as retaliation from the former lover, gossip in the profession, and a sense of fear and humiliation at work.

May graduate students date other students?

Yes. This happens all the time. Many people attend graduate school just at the age when their friends are finding mates and settling down. Graduate school, especially during the coursework phase, is a particularly intense experience that throws together people of similar interests and dispositions. Building both friendships and romantic relationships is a natural consequence of immersion in the graduate school environment. Graduate students are peers without important professional power differentials; hence, the ethical provisions that make student-faculty relationships unacceptable do not apply. But structuring a life around both careers of two academic partners presents its own considerable challenges.

Why do some graduate students live apart from their partners?

In order to achieve their education and career goals, many academics live apart from their partners for some time, ranging from, at one end of the scale, a couple of months or a few years to permanently at the other end. Academics whose partners are nonacademic professionals are not immune from this hardship, but the shape of the job market makes it especially common in relationships where both partners are academics. Graduate students who fall in love with each other while at the same university may find it difficult to fine appropriate jobs in the same locale later. Depending on their resources and the distance between their home bases, partners who live apart may see each other relatively frequently (as often as every weekend) or rarely (only between semesters). Strategies for ameliorating the strains of such long-distance relationships include talking on the phone or Skype, e-mail, and banning work during time together.

Why live apart rather than together? So that each can have the career that matters to them. Academic degree programs and jobs are neither clustered so closely together nor so easy to obtain that partners can simply identify the place they want to live together and decide to find jobs there. It may take several years of living apart before partners can build up their status to the point where they have the leverage to find jobs in the same town. Often one partner decides to lower his or her career aspirations, or give them up altogether, rather than continuing to live apart. Couples with children find this problem excruciating since most parental responsibilities fall on one partner while the other partner misses seeing the children grow up.

The problem of finding two jobs in the same locale is commonly referred to as "the two-body problem."

What challenges do parents of young children face in graduate school?

Female graduate students may spend their most fertile years in graduate school and then, if lucky, on the tenure track. When, they wonder, will I ever get to have a child?

For many professionals, there is never an ideal time to reproduce. The pressures are especially acute for women in the academy, whose prime childbearing years often correspond precisely to the stress-filled years of completing a graduate degree, finding a job, and meeting the requirements for tenure. A young woman who begins graduate school within a few years of graduating from college, finishes up in relatively short order (say, six years), wins a tenure-track job after only one or two years on the job market, and achieves tenure on schedule without changing jobs (again, six years), will find herself in her late thirties before the pressure is sufficiently eased for her to have a child without jeopardizing her career. In her late thirties, however, the risks of infertility and various birth defects increase, making this an unattractive (though not impossible) time to start having children. A woman who begins graduate school in her late twenties and takes longer to write her dissertation or find a job may find herself well beyond her fertile years before she is tenured.

Consequently many women pursuing academic careers who desire children opt to have them as graduate students, while on the job market, or on the tenure track. None of these options is easy; each choice presents its own difficulties that women in this situation must figure out how to negotiate.

Graduate students who have children enjoy much time and flexibility in arranging their care, but they do so while living on relatively meager departmental stipends (if there is one). Day care costs can eat up a student's entire stipend. Parents of young children also have to figure out how to manage the time necessary for intensive research (possibly including travel to places abroad or for other reasons inhospitable to children) and writing.

Women who go on the job market worry that search committees will reject them out of hand if they are visibly pregnant or make inquiries about local childcare arrangements. Never mind that hiring discrimination on such grounds is illegal and unwise and that this is the twenty-first century; they worry anyway.

Tenure-track faculty often burn the midnight oil preparing

> **VOICE:**
> We go to a place that expects you to take your academic life to be all you have. When you know that your profs would be upset if you got married or pregnant you look at how you spend your time and how much you work a little differently. . . . Profs at my school got mad at girls who got pregnant. They didn't think it was right to do when a grad student.
>
> —Merce, re "Why is grad school so hard?"

classes and doing the reading and writing necessary for tenure. They worry that they may not be able to parent responsibly or well, as of course they want to do, under such pressures.

The pressures and considerations remain different for men, who do not put their bodies on the line to bear children and who still, for the most part, do not assume most of the responsibility for child-rearing. To some extent, however, many of the above considerations worry male academics as well.

In none of these situations is it impossible to have children or raise them well. Nor is it necessarily more difficult for academics to combine family and work than it is for other professionals. But being observant types, graduate students are often so aware of the risks to their careers or their parenting abilities that they postpone having children. To this day, many academic women never have children.

Degrees, Jobs, and Academic Careers

O ne of my friends from graduate school got a great job as an assistant professor at exactly the university she wanted to spend her career in. She solved the two-body problem and found a job in the same city as her partner. Her teenage children adjusted well to the move. She attracted interesting graduate students and worked on her research. She proudly showed her mother her first journal article, published in a prestigious journal. Her mother's response was horror. "How," she asked "can they still make you write papers now that you have finished your doctorate?" My friend patiently explained that she had been trained to read and think and write, and that she was delighted to have obtained a job where she would be paid to do those things.

In many ways, earning a doctoral degree sets a graduate student up to do more of what she has already been doing for years—reading books and articles, asking scholarly questions, conducting research, writing papers, and teaching. The authors of a recent large survey of doctoral students in the United States found that more than one-half of students in the humanities, social sciences, and sciences aspire to academic positions, while around a one-third of engineering and education students had similar hopes.[1] Being a professor is one way to put the skills cultivated in graduate school to work professionally, but it is not the only way. Moving from graduate school to "the real world," however, is no more straightforward than the process of writing a dissertation. Graduate students must decide whether to look for an academic job or one outside the academy. If they want a teaching position, they need to figure out what kind of school to try for and then learn how to pursue that goal effectively. This chapter sketches the kinds of choice that new graduates make as they confront their futures.

What are the employment prospects of a newly minted Ph.D.?

The academic job market for Ph.D.s varies considerably by field, but a realistic overall characterization, even in good economic times, is "mostly terrible." For several decades, U.S. universities have been turning out many more people with Ph.D.s than there are tenure-track jobs available. While most people who earn professional degrees can find work in their chosen field (even if it turns out that they do not like it very much or they are not very good at it), a Ph.D. is no guarantee of the primary job for which it trains a student: a position as a professor. Aspiring to be a professor is a little like hoping to make the NFL: it is very hard, and most hopefuls do not make it, so if one is going to try it really helps to enjoy playing the game for its intrinsic rewards.

In addition, the job market is stratified in curious ways. The people with the most prestigious degrees are not necessarily the ones who find jobs. Colleges and universities tend to hire prospective faculty whose profiles fit the local institutional culture. Research universities, to be sure, prefer to hire Ph.D.s from the most elite institutions. But teaching-focused universities, liberal arts colleges, and community colleges often hesitate to hire new faculty members who look like they intend to put all their energies into research at the expense of teaching or who will leave for greener pastures shortly after starting the job. The magazine for historians in the United States recently observed that hiring trends "suggested that the smaller and less prestigious programs serve a vital niche market—feeding faculty into positions at small two- and four-year institutions, particularly in the interior of the country, which students from elite programs would not consider."[2] So a Ph.D. with an adequate but not stellar dissertation written at a mid-tier university might well beat out an Ivy League star for a job at a small college in Iowa. Despite the guidance offered by many graduate programs, the academic job market is not a pure research meritocracy.

In general, the job market is worst in the humanities. As few as one-half of people with Ph.D.s in fields like English and history end up teaching at the college level, and many of these never secure tenure-track positions. Social scientists and natural scientists are more likely to find work as professors, if they choose, though scientists in particular may find private-sector work at their fingertips. A few fields are trendy enough that the supply of potential faculty members is smaller than the number of job openings. Recently, in the early twenty-first century, for example, accounting has been a hot field.

Fortunately, someone who is smart enough and works hard enough to earn a Ph.D. has many transferrable skills. For students who want to transition out of the academy, the university career office can facilitate learning about other employment options and connect them with job prospects. The norms for applying for and

---

VOICE:

I don't think grad school is hard if you just want the degree. If you want to use the degree for an academic career, then surprises may be in store. The biggest shock is that no one gives a hoot how hard you try; it is what you PRODUCE. By the time you are finished with grad school, you are supposed to have some teaching experience, some publications, and maybe even attempts at grant writing. No one will care how many tier 1 peer-reviewed papers you TRIED to publish, it only matters how many you DID publish. Many "brilliant" undergrads become average, and some OK undergrads will become stellar grad students. This disturbs some former undergrads who were used to being "good students." Being a good student does not count for much, being a good scholar will. Hand-holding diminishes, and you have to have your own drive to keep going, which is why many doc[toral] students remain ABD.

—Shamu, re "Why is grad school so hard?"

winning nonacademic jobs are different from those that prevail in the academy, but they are no more inaccessible or mysterious.

What are the steps in the academic hiring process?

Compared with most other professional job markets, the academic hiring process is painfully slow, running on an annual cycle that corresponds to the academic year. Because colleges and universities look to hire people who will ultimately earn tenure, and therefore be around for decades, they make hiring decisions with deliberation, but at a snail's pace.

The first stage is the creation of the job opportunity. Colleges and universities typically know by April or May the kinds of jobs they want to start advertising for in September. Departments use the summer and early fall to persuade administrators to let them hire and to craft suitable job announcements. Job ads tend to request that applicants submit their materials to search committees in the fall semester. In late December, faculty are furiously busy grading final exams and papers and so search committees hope to screen applications in November.

Materials typically requested include a cover letter, a CV, several reference letters, and a writing sample of about 30 pages. Some departments also ask applicants to submit teaching portfolios. It is noteworthy that transcripts are absent from this list. A hiring institution may eventually conduct a background check that includes verification of the finalist's credentials, but academic search committees do not use graduate student grades as a way to figure out whom to hire: what matters is the research, as represented by the dissertation and publications, and the candidate's teaching record or portfolio.

After scrutinizing applicants' documentation to determine who best fits their position's profile (which may have evolved since the job was advertised), the search committee develops a "long list" of candidates to study in greater depth. They may request additional writing samples and references or move straight to preliminary interviews. In fields like history and literature, these interviews usually occur at the giant national conferences held around the new year. Another common method for whittling a long list down to a short list is to conduct phone or Skype interviews. In both these approaches, the search committee spends a long day together in a small room, having half-hour-long conversations with prospective colleagues. The content of the interviews varies with the values of the hiring department, but in general the conversations are two-way streets. The search committee tries to sell their school as a place where a candidate would like to come and work, and the interviewee, of course, tries to make herself sound like the perfect match for the job. Once the spring semester starts up, the search committee's job is to narrow the list of candidates down to three or four who will be invited to campus for a day-long interview.

The campus visit is a very long day for the candidate. Typical activities include several meals with prospective colleagues, a meeting with students, one or two presentations, a campus tour, and a meeting with the dean (who later will extend the formal job offer); at small colleges, the president may also interview job candidates. The presentations are the key to deciding who gets hired. At most institutions, the "job talk" consists of a lecture about the candidate's research, followed by a question-and-answer session. Some institutions that emphasize teaching may ask candidates to teach a class—either a group of real students or faculty pretending to be students. The treatment of the candidate during these talks depends on departmental culture. At some places, being interrogated and treated to a head-spinning round of critique is a sign of respect, while at other places candidates are handled more gently. In my department, we ask softball questions to candidates who are clearly floundering. At the best job talk I ever witnessed, a cranky senior faculty member growled and complained when the candidate started explaining research that was covered in his writing sample. Rather than bore his prospective colleagues by repeating what they had already read, he ditched his notes and spoke extemporaneously about a different project.

By the time all the on-campus interviews are through, it might be late February. After all the candidates have visited campus, the search committee and hiring department decide whom they want to hire and ask the dean to extend an offer. The process often gets combative at this point. Perhaps the department is conflicted about who was the best candidate. Perhaps the department and dean disagree. Eventually the decision is made; if there was no internal deadlock (which does occur), an offer is extended.

There are some discipline-specific variations in this process. In economics, for example, faculty at the highest-caliber departments rank their own graduate students on the job market and parcel them out to hiring institutions accordingly. Disciplines like geography and sociology, whose major conferences do not fall neatly between the application-collection season and the on-campus interview period, find some other way, such as the telephone, to conduct preliminary interviews.

This process leads to an unfortunate sense that anyone still on the job market in April—which is always the case since there is an oversupply of job seekers—is a leftover, a reject, implicitly flawed, since they were not good enough to get a job during the normal cycle. The flip side of this coin is that jobs listed late in the academic year, too, are looked at askance: what kind of college cannot get its act together in time to hire when the most promising candidates are still on the market? Job candidates and hiring departments who can get over these prejudices often are able to make happy, last-minute matches.

What is the difference between a résumé and a curriculum vitae, or CV?

Both CVs and résumés are basic documents used in job hunting to represent a person's educational and employment history. But while résumés tend to be short and tailored toward a job seeker's next opportunity, CVs are detailed histories of everything that an academic has accomplished over the course of her career, including publications, presentations, awards, grants, and professional service. Scholars may possess short versions of their CVs for specific narrow purposes (such as illustrating their basic credentials in a grant proposal), but when they apply for an academic job they submit the long version, so that prospective employers can see both the breadth and depth of their professional accomplishments.

What are the rhythms of the academic job market?

It is perfectly normal for it to take a year to fill a tenure-track faculty position. There are several reasons, some institutional, some cultural, that explain the dilatory pace of academic hiring.

For the applicant, a new job can be life-changing. But it is also potentially life-changing for an academic department. Some larger departments are used to losing colleagues to other institutions and hiring new members every year, but a small department might have permission to search for candidates only once every decade or so. When a department extends a job offer, it may be inviting someone who will spend the rest of his career in the office next door. Such a decision deserves careful review.

In addition, budgetary and administrative constraints govern hiring cycles. Conducting a search can be expensive. Candidates often must travel great distances to visit the school for a day or so, and most colleges and universities cover the travel expenses of interviewees; community colleges, however, often do not do so. If a department runs through its search budget before finding a candidate that the department and the dean (and other officials) can agree on, or if the candidates who are offered positions decline them, the search is usually called a failure, to be restarted the next academic year when there is new money in the budget for further advertising and travel. Administrators may reason that if none of the top three interviewed candidates works out, they have gone too deep in the pool.

Because it is a hirers' market, with many more people qualified to teach at college level than there are available tenure-track positions, institutions can afford to be choosy and slow. If a search fails or is delayed a year or two, it is easy and inexpensive to find adjunct teachers or visiting assistant professors to teach until a permanent colleague is found.

Should a prospective professor pick a place where she wants to live and then focus her job search there?

Many Americans thinking about their career prospects consider where they want to live as carefully as they consider how they want to spend their work time. Some desire to live in a particular city or appealing region of the country so they can pursue a favorite leisure activity: they limit their job search to Colorado to be guaranteed a great ski season, for example. Others plan to live in their hometown or near to extended family so that their children will grow up knowing their kin; yet others want to live in an exciting big city while they search for a mate; and some want nothing more than to nest in an old farmhouse and spend weekends renovating it.

However, only a lucky few academics are able, at least in the short run, to choose both home and job. Unfortunately, most prospective faculty find that the (inter)national character of the academic job market precludes being able to choose both job and location.

When colleges and universities decide to open a position, they often have in mind very specific characteristics that they want from their new colleague: the ability to teach particular courses or expertise in a very specialized research field. Most institutions in fact hire new faculty in a particular field only relatively rarely, which makes the chances of a graduate student's readiness for the job market coinciding with the perfect job opening up in a desired locale quite remote. Given time, it is possible that the right job in the right place will open up, but by then other factors may have intervened so that what might at an earlier time have been the perfect job may no longer fit the bill: the aspirant may have become invested in her new home; her research interests may have shifted; the location might be right, but the job listing be for an entry-level assistant professor, while in the meantime she has been promoted to full professor.

In view of all this, graduate students who must live in a particular location might decide to let place be the deciding factor even if it

---

VOICE:

One of the very worst sides of academia is how difficult it is—virtually impossible, really—to find a job in one's discipline in a specific geographical area. You have to be willing to take a job wherever it may turn out to be. Viewed from up close, that's just a fact of life, but when you compare academia to other job tracks available to a talented young person—becoming a doctor, a lawyer, a computer programmer—this is most definitely a down side.

—John Goldsmith in *The Chicago Guide to Your Academic Career* means giving up the dream of the tenure track. The odds of success are best for faculty who want to live in a big city that has many colleges and universities: one of them, some day, might have the right position available at the right time.

Do academic careers have to begin with an assistant professorship?

In most fields, yes. The most important way of demonstrating suitability for tenure is by producing the appropriate scholarship and gaining experience teaching. Assistant professor positions are structured to permit a tenure candidate to accomplish these tasks at the required levels of excellence. In the sciences, however, it is possible to start out in industry or government and slide into a starting or even tenured position after many years outside the academy. Peter Feibelman advises scientists to avoid starting as assistant professors: such positions come with low pay, long hours, and a future that includes the make-or-break decision of tenure.[3]

Why do women still leave the academy disproportionately?

The rate at which women drop out of the academy worries some observers. While many women view the academy as an excellent place to work, others encounter obstacles they regard as unacceptable. The number of tenured women academics has increased in recent decades, but in most fields, especially the sciences, men remain disproportionately represented in the ranks of the tenured.

For some women, the autonomy and flexibility of academic life perfectly suits their priorities. What other women notice, however, is that the climb toward tenure coincides directly with the period of decreasing fertility or conflicts with their family's needs. Some stay, but others choose to put their skills to use elsewhere. Additionally, some women experience gender discrimination. In 2005, Harvard University President Lawrence Summers notoriously encapsulated the barriers that academic women continue to face when he publicly suggested that most women do not have what it takes to succeed in research science.

Do universities hire their own Ph.D.s as faculty?

Universities almost never hire their own graduates to the tenure track. Advanced graduate students and recent Ph.D.s often make up a large portion of the adjunct faculty at their alma maters, but hiring someone permanently is considered a bad idea. The presumption against a university hiring its own graduates is rooted in the idea that a rich intellectual environment requires regular infusion of new ideas and scholarship from the outside. It may also feel socially awkward for established faculty members to accept their former students as peers and colleagues.

There are three exceptions to this general rule, all of them rare. In some instances, a graduate of one program at an institution is hired by a department other than the one where she did her graduate work. This happens infrequently because graduate programs tend to be so highly specialized that a student trained in one discipline is not usually qualified to teach in another program. The second circumstance is that a recent Ph.D. goes away to teach somewhere else for several years and then is hired back at his alma mater. The third case occurs when an institution trains someone who is obviously the most brilliant person to come along in the discipline in the last decade or so. That star, they keep—if they can.

What is spousal hiring?

Increasingly in the twenty-first century, universities and colleges recognize the two-body problem as an opportunity to build their faculties. By hiring both halves of an academic couple, a college can keep a talented faculty member from leaving for another institution. Often the "trailing spouse" is as good a scholar and teacher as the one who received the initial job offer. For many reasons, however, significant resistance to partner hiring remains, making inquiries into an institution's spousal hiring practices politically delicate.

What is a postdoc?

Postdoctoral jobs are positions that students become eligible for after they complete their Ph.D.s. The word *postdoc* refers both to the position and the person holding it. Postdocs are typically hired at research universities by faculty members running large laboratories supported by grant money. A few nongrant-based positions are supported by institutions cultivating scholarship in particular disciplines. Usually, postdocs' responsibilities consist entirely of research, although sometimes they have the opportunity to teach as well.

The postdoc is an intermediate position in the academic career ladder. Although sometimes referred to as "postdoctoral students," postdocs are more employees than they are students (though they are often learning new things in their research). The faculty member who hires the postdoc is both boss and mentor, and the employer's recommendation is critical to the postdoc's ability to find a subsequent, more senior, permanent academic position such as an assistant professorship. A Ph.D. might take several postdocs sequentially before settling into a stable position.

Postdoctoral positions are much more common in the natural sciences than they are in other academic disciplines, in large part because scientists routinely bring large sums of grant money into the university to fund their research projects. For a scientist to obtain a faculty position at a research university, postdoctoral experience is essential. For science Ph.D.s who hope to work at colleges that are more focused on teaching, having held at least one postdoc position is highly desirable, though not absolutely critical. Postdocs are also available in the humanities and social sciences, but they are not considered prerequisites to a tenure-track position. A postdoc can, however, keep a former graduate student gainfully employed while he enjoys several extra years to test out the job market and the opportunity to devote himself to research instead of teaching and service.

How likely are faculty members to change jobs?

Professors do change jobs, but tenured professors do not move on at the same rate as the rest of the population. For many scholars, a first academic job is a position as an adjunct faculty member, a one-year position replacing a professor on sabbatical, or a postdoc. None of these jobs is likely to become permanent. An academic who takes a job as an assistant professor may settle down permanently. But if she wants to move—to a more congenial department, a more hospitable location, or up the academic hierarchy—she has to do so within a few years. Because untenured faculty earn the lowest salaries, most permanent positions are advertised at the level of assistant professor. Jobs for tenured faculty are available, as are administrative positions for which only senior scholars are eligible, but they are relatively few and far between.

Can a professor at a community college hope to land a job in the Ivy League?

I once heard an apocryphal story suggesting that is possible to "write your way out" of a job at a community college—the bottom of the academic hierarchy—into one at the top of the ladder. But I heard it only the one time. Community colleges and research universities hire entirely different kinds of scholars, making it unlikely that one person's profile would appeal to search committees at such different institutions. Although the tightness of the job market means that increasingly community colleges can demand that faculty have earned doctorates, they hire people who are dedicated exclusively to teaching. Faculty at research institutions may be good teachers, but they must focus on their research to be successful. A stellar scholar who takes a faculty job at a community college is likely to be kept so busy teaching five classes a semester that she cannot make the time to publish at a rate that would make her attractive to a research institution.

Why does writing a dissertation qualify a graduate student to be a professor?

Teaching at the primary or secondary school level requires expertise in pedagogy. Especially in public schools, teachers must have earned a specified number of credits in education. At the college and university level, by contrast, what counts is subject-area expertise, particularly the ability to produce new knowledge, as demonstrated by writing a dissertation. New assistant professors may have little knowledge of teaching strategies or even no classroom experience the first time they face a room of undergraduates (although in this era the job market is so tight that colleges can demand that new faculty do have prior teaching experience). This situation prevails even though almost all professors work as teachers and only some continue as active researchers throughout their careers. The rationale for allowing untrained teachers into the college classroom is that what is taught is high-level knowledge of certain subjects, and that only someone with a deep-enough understanding of an area to produce new scholarship in that area is able to synthesize it effectively. It also helps that college students are (presumptive) adults and do not need the same kind of external discipline that children require.

How do new professors learn to be teachers?

Would-be teachers in primary and secondary schools go to school to learn to be educators. They take classes in child development, learn about educational theory, and have practice teaching apprenticeships before they are hired. Professors, by contrast, learn on the job. It is entirely possible for a star researcher with no teaching experience to win a tenure-track position. Possible, though not completely likely. Most graduate students, especially those in the humanities and social sciences, work as teaching assistants or adjunct faculty as a way of financing their educations. Even so, academics learn by doing rather than from educational theory or mentoring. Similarly, new tenure-track faculty often spend their first couple of years on the job figuring out how to balance the demands of preparing classes they have never taught before with their other service and research responsibilities.

Do professors spend as much time on research as graduate students do?

Graduate students who succeed have to spend time on their research. There is no route to a Ph.D. without research. Professors, some of whom are hired exclusively to teach, can get away without researching for years at a time. But many faculty positions are structured to encourage research. Professors write grant proposals and take sabbaticals from teaching so that they can focus on their scholarship without interruption. During the academic year, a professor might spend the majority of his time working on his teaching, and then devote the summer to reading and writing. How much time professors spend on research depends on their jobs and their professional ambitions.

What do professors do in the summer?

On one level, professors are only "on duty" during the September to May academic year, when they have to show up regularly in classrooms. Only a few programs require their faculty to teach summer session regularly; education departments, for example, need their faculty to be available in summer because that is the time when primary and secondary school teachers seek continuing education credits. On another, level, however, professors' jobs are much more demanding than a nine-month schedule suggests. In addition to appearing in the classroom, faculty have to prepare new courses and revise existing classes, perform service for their institution and profession, and, often, engage in ongoing research projects. These responsibilities routinely spill over into the summer.

As a consequence of the fiction that professors work only during the school year, they are usually paid only during the academic year, receiving no compensation during the summer. One scholar notes, "If you are not bringing in substantial outside funding your nine months' pay will not be particularly generous."[4] Some institutions and banks make it possible for professors to set aside a portion of their monthly income for redistribution in the summer, but some scholars (especially those who have accumulated debt on credit cards or who have substantial student loans) find it difficult to spread their nine-month salaries over the entire year. To make up that deficit or to achieve other financial goals, professors sometimes agree to teach during the summer session or the increasingly popu-

VOICE:
The flexibility of the academic schedule is wrapped around a core of inflexibility: that core is the hours during which your courses are scheduled. There are few reasons acceptable for canceling a class. If you are home sick in bed, that's one; but in general, having a child home sick in bed is not a valid reason to cancel a class. Cancel an appointment, yes, or office hours.

—John Goldsmith in *The Chicago Guide to Your Academic Career*

lar "winter term," the time between the start of the year and the beginning of the spring semester.

Are professors satisfied with their work?

Professors, like other people, love, hate, and are indifferent to their work. But for some people and some fields, the work of scholarship nourishes the soul. The *Wall Street Journal* recently reported a survey of the best and worst jobs in the United States. Although the occupation of professor was not broken out as a separate category, biologist, historian, and mathematician ranked as fourth, fifth, and sixth best on the list. Sociologists, astronomers, economists, and physicists were not as high on the satisfaction list as dental hygienists or financial planners, but all ranked in the top 30.[5]

What nonacademic careers are open to Ph.D.s?

A former graduate student may have aged out of eligibility for military service or a career in professional sports, but he can probably do almost anything else. It is hard to imagine a job that an advanced degree disqualifies one for. Higher education is designed to improve students' research, reasoning, and writing abilities, all qualities that are valuable in nonacademic professional careers. The bad news is that because many nonacademic employers seek to hire people with job-specific skills or knowledge, former graduate students may have to retrain or take entry-level jobs in order to come up to speed in their new fields.

How can Ph.D.s persuade nonacademic employers to hire them?

The skills that graduate students learn—research, reasoning, and writing—are certainly transferable to many other areas of work. But graduate students have not always learned the specific content that nonacademic employers are looking for or how to express their skills in terms appealing to the business world. Advanced academic programs, which teach students how to create new knowledge and ideas in highly specialized or even arcane areas, tend not to supply students with information that is directly applicable to established areas of work. Therefore employers may ignore, or even view as a deficit, the presence of a master's degree or Ph.D. on a résumé. Graduate students and Ph.D.s looking for work beyond the academy should consult their university's career center for advice on how to present their hard-won skills in terms that nonacademic employers will value.

A marvelous resource for graduate students considering nonacademic careers is Susan Basalla and Maggie Debelius's *"So What Are You Going to Do with That?" Finding Careers Outside Academia.*[6] The authors interviewed hundreds of former graduate students and explain how people with advanced degrees can market themselves to employers. One of their key points is that every graduate student should have a plan B that they cultivate while pursuing the degree. Students should keep up hobbies, volunteer work, and nonacademic networks that will enable them to slip back into the "real world" if the academy does not pan out. Jerald Jellison's *Life after Grad School* provides an overview of how to make the transition from academics to business, with an emphasis on interpreting academic skills to business employers.[7]

Afterword

One of my students had a miserable first semester in graduate school and working as a teaching assistant. The professor she was working for terrified her. Another instructor yelled at her in front of her students when she overstayed her allotted time in her classroom by one minute. She caught a stomach bug from sitting in the same classroom with me after I foolishly decided to teach my graduate seminar while ill. She was in a bike accident and later that bike broke for good. She was robbed at gunpoint. The classes she was hoping to get into for the second semester were filled up. A young man broke her heart. Yet she finished out her coursework with a smile on her face, told me she still loved graduate school, and looked eagerly forward to more. She, I am confident, will have a happy academic career. Her irrepressible nature and her love for the work itself will sustain her through the inevitable rough spots.

If graduate school requires so much work with so little reward, why would anyone bother?

Humans are driven. We are programmed to breathe, to eat, to sleep, to reproduce, and to learn. The urge to learn more than the minimum is not universal, but for some of us, the impulse to discover is as basic as the drive for sex. We cannot imagine any way to spend our days that is more fun than research. Nothing can substitute for the joy of exploring new ideas, the satisfaction of discovery, and the pride in communicating new knowledge to others.

Many people do lead fulfilling lives, lives enhanced by reading, conversation, and exploration of interesting ideas, all without going to graduate school. Earning a master's degree or a doctorate requires sacrifices and stamina that do not make sense for everyone. Going to graduate school is most worthwhile for someone who craves the ability to make sense of a portion of the world that no one else has previously comprehended. Graduate school harnesses our intelligence, our discipline, our skills, and cultivates our capacity to understand the universe. Go to graduate school, but only if you must.

Notes

....

Preface

1. Nathan E. Bell, "Graduate Enrollment and Degrees: 1999 to 2009" (Washington, DC: Council of Graduate Schools, 2010), www.cgsnet.org/portals/o/pdf/R_ED2009.pdf; accessed Jan. 7, 2011, 22.

2. The surveys were approved by UWM's Institutional Review Board. To protect respondent privacy, when I quote from their accounts I suppress most identifying information and have not offered detailed citations. I have followed the same practice in recounting the stories of my friends and students.

Chapter Two: Financing Your Education

1. "College Families Going Hungry," *Calgary Herald*, Canada.com, Nov. 20, 2006.

Chapter Three: Graduate Expectations

1. J. Wesley McWhorter, Harvey Wallmann, and Richard D. Tandy, "An Evaluation of Physical Fitness Parameters for Graduate Students," *Journal of American College Health* 51 (2002): 32–37.

2. William G. Bowen and Neil L. Rudenstein, *In Pursuit of the PhD* (Princeton, NJ: Princeton University Press, 1992), 116.

3. Michael T. Nettles and Catherine M. Millett, *Three Magic Letters: Getting to Ph.D.* (Baltimore: Johns Hopkins University Press, 2006), xx.

4. Ronald G. Ehrenberg, Harriet Zuckerman, Jeffrey A. Groen, and Sharon M. Brucker, *Educating Scholars: Doctoral Education in the Humanities* (Princeton, NJ: Princeton University Press, 2010), 5.

5. Robert L. Peters, *Getting What You Came For: The Smart Student's Guide to Earning a Master's or Ph.D.*, rev. ed. (New York: Noonday Press, 1997), 186.

6. Dale F. Bloom, Jonathan D. Karp, and Nicholas Cohen, *The Ph.D. Process: A Student's Guide to Graduate School in the Sciences* (New York: Oxford University Press, 1998), 56.

7. Nettles and Millett, *Three Magic Letters*, 131.

8. Bowen and Rudenstine, *In Pursuit*, 105; emphasis in the original.

9. Susan Basalla and Maggie Debelius, *"So What Are You Going to Do with That?" Finding Careers outside Academia*, rev. ed. (Chicago: University of Chicago Press, 2007; originally published as *"So What Are You Going to Do with That?" A Guide to Career-Changing for M.A.'s and Ph.D.'s*, Farrar, Straus & Giroux, 2001), 14.

Chapter Four: Coursework Is Hard Work

1. Dale F. Bloom, Jonathan D. Karp, and Nicholas Cohen, *The Ph.D. Process: A Student's Guide to Graduate School in the Sciences* (New York: Oxford University Press, 1998), 80.

2. Michael T. Nettles and Catherine M. Millett, *Three Magic Letters: Getting to Ph.D.* (Baltimore: Johns Hopkins University Press, 2006), 119.

3. Nettles and Millett, *Three Magic Letters*, 118.

4. Bloom, Karp, and Cohen, *Ph.D. Process*, 36.

5. Peter J. Feibelman, *A Ph.D. Is Not Enough: A Guide to Survival in Science* (Reading, MA: Addison-Wesley, 1993), 30.

Chapter Five: Dissertations and Theses

1. Peter J. Feibelman, *A Ph.D. Is Not Enough: A Guide to Survival in Science* (Reading, MA: Addison-Wesley, 1993), 45.

2. Barbara Rittner and Patricia Trudeau, *The Women's Guide to Surviving Graduate School* (Thousand Oaks, CA: Sage, 1997), 7.

Chapter Six: The Academic Culture

1. Michael T. Nettles and Catherine M. Millett, *Three Magic Letters: Getting to Ph.D.* (Baltimore: Johns Hopkins University Press, 2006), 183.

2. "Games People Play with Authors' Names," *Nature* 387, no. 6636 (1997): 831.

3. R. A. Alpher, H. Bethe, and G. Gamow, "The Origin of Chemical Elements," *Physical Review* 73 (1948): 803–4. The story is recounted in "Ralph Ascher Alpher," http://en.wikipedia.org/wiki/Ralph_Alpher; accessed Jan. 21, 2011.

4. Johns Hopkins University Press, "Some Questions about the Publishing Contract: A Guide for Authors," adapted from Weldon A. Kefauver, *Scholars and Their Publishers* (New York: Modern Language Association of America, 1977), 3.

5. Nettles and Millett, *Three Magic Letters*, 172.

Chapter Seven: Having a Life in Graduate School

1. Susan Basalla and Maggie Debelius, *"So What Are You Going to Do with That?" Finding Careers Outside Academia*, rev. ed. (Chicago: University of Chicago Press, 2007).

2. Jerald M. Jellison, *Life after Grad School: Getting from A to B* (Oxford: Oxford University Press, 2010).

Chapter Eight: Degrees, Jobs, and Academic Careers

1. Michael T. Nettles and Catherine M. Millett, *Three Magic Letters: Getting to Ph.D.* (Baltimore: Johns Hopkins University Press, 2006), xix.

2. Robert B. Townsend, "NRC Report Provides Data on History Doctoral Programs," *Perspectives on History* (Dec. 2010): 14.

3. Peter J. Feibelman, *A Ph.D. Is Not Enough: A Guide to Survival in Science* (Reading, MA: Addison-Wesley, 1993), 59.

4. Feibelman, *Ph.D. Is Not Enough*, 58.

5. "Best and Worst Jobs 2010," Jan. 5, 2010, *Wall Street Journal*, http://online.wsj.com/public/resources/documents/st_BESTJOBS2010_20100105.html; accessed Jan. 29, 2010.

6. Susan Basalla and Maggie Debelius, *"So What Are You Going to Do with That?" Finding Careers Outside Academia*, rev. ed. (Chicago: University of Chicago Press, 2007).

7. Jerald M. Jellison, *Life after Grad School: Getting from A to B* (Oxford: Oxford University Press, 2010).

Glossary

....

ABD (All But Dissertation): A person who has completed all coursework and exams required preliminary to launching on the dissertation proposal, research, and writing. The ABD student has started but not yet finished the dissertation. A former graduate student who never completed the dissertation is sometimes referred to as "a permanent ABD."

The academy: Shorthand for the collective enterprise of higher education, including research, writing, professional relationships, and graduate training.

Carnegie Classifications: A system for categorizing institutions of higher education in the United States developed by the Carnegie Commission on Higher Education. The original rating system classified colleges and universities by their research productivity and the kinds of degrees they offered. In 2005, the system of description was substantially changed, but the older terms, such as "Research I" (RI) to describe the top tier of universities, remain part of common academic parlance.

Curriculum vitae (CV): The academic version of a résumé. In contrast to the kind of document required to apply for a job in "the real world," a CV tends to list all of the scholar's credentials, including publications, courses taught, papers given, and awards. For some purposes, scholars use a short version of the CV that highlights only major accomplishments. The term itself is Latin for "Course of Life." Academics unfamiliar with Latin sometimes mistakenly leave the final *e* off of *vitae*. See also **Real world.**

Dissertator: A graduate student who is working on a dissertation proposal or dissertation, having completed all other requirements for the doctoral degree.

Doctoral candidate: An official status granted by a university to a graduate student who has completed a set of minimum requirements toward the doctorate, usually all coursework and required exams. A student achieving this status is sometimes referred to as having been "admitted to candidacy" for the doctorate and often qualifies for a reduced rate of tuition. At some graduation ceremonies, students about to receive their degrees are announced as "candidates for the degree."

Doctoral student: A graduate student working toward a doctorate at any stage of the process. The distinction between doctoral candidates and doctoral students is important, with candidates being closer to completing the degree.

GPA (Grade Point Average): Figure representing a student's overall achievement of class grades. It is usually calculated on a 4.0 scale. An A is worth four points and a D is worth one.

Graduate faculty: Faculty members who are permitted by institutional standards to advise graduate students and teach graduate courses. Faculty members who have not completed their own Ph.D.s, for example, might be prohibited from teaching graduate students until their own dissertations have been filed with their home institutions. People who teach in a department as adjunct or temporary staff are typically excluded from the graduate faculty.

IRB (Institutional Review Board): A committee empowered to make sure that scholarly research conducted by faculty, staff, and students is designed to minimize risk and harm to human subjects. Planned projects ranging from testing of medical procedures and therapies to surveys and oral histories are subject to approval by the IRB. Researchers also may use the term IRB to refer to the paperwork they must submit to this committee.

Peer review: The process by which scholarship is judged fit for publication by most academic journals and university presses. Scholars in the research field of the article or book assess its strengths, weaknesses, and suitability for publication in the venue to which it was submitted. In some cases, such as books, the reviewers know the identity of the author; in the case of articles, the writer's name is usually kept secret. Authors are only rarely informed of the names of their reviewers so that reviewers will feel free to be completely candid in their assessments.

Postdoc: A research job in the laboratory of an established faculty member held after completion of the dissertation but before finding permanent work as a professor or in the private sector. Postdocs are common in the sciences and relatively rare in the humanities and social sciences.

Principal investigator (PI): In research projects conducted by groups of scholars, the principal investigator is the lead author and overseer of all the work. The PI is the one who submits grant applications, makes decisions about staffing, and receives the most credit for the resulting publications. Graduate students and postdocs who work in multiresearcher laboratories in the sciences often can list themselves as secondary authors on lots of publications, but their CVs mark them as capable of leading research when they are credited as PI on at least one project.

Real world: The (somewhat) tongue-in-cheek label given to life, especially paid work, beyond the academy. Used both to admonish lazy undergraduates ("when you get out in the real world you won't be able to skip work the way you skip class") and to bemoan the shortcomings of academic life ("salaries in the real world reflect a person's education level much better than those in the academy").

Residency requirements: Regulations imposed by the university that require students to enroll continuously in a certain number of courses over a specified stretch of time. The idea behind residency requirements is that graduate study is more than coursework; rather, it includes immersion in the culture of an institution and a profession as well as familiarity with the products of scholarly knowledge.

SLAC: A small, or selective, liberal arts college. For the most part, SLACs do not offer graduate degrees. But their faculties are peopled by Ph.D.s. Some SLACs encourage their faculty to continue to conduct the kind of original research required for the doctoral degree; others reward their faculty for pursuing excellence in teaching.

Tenure: The right of a professor to hold his or her job permanently. A tenured professor is in this way enabled to speak her mind in classroom and scholarship without fear of retribution in the form of job loss. Granted at most colleges and universities to faculty who have met a set of minimum requirements, including approximately six years at the level of assistant professor and an affirmative vote from colleagues and superiors.

Terminal degree: The highest earned degree in a given field, the terminal degree is frequently the minimum requirement for a faculty position. For most of the traditional academic disciplines, this degree is a Ph.D. In some disciplines, the terminal degree is some other form of doctorate or a master's degree such as a master in fine arts.

Terminal master's: a master's degree awarded to a student without the implication that she is prepared to pursue a terminal doctorate. For example, a student who opted to take an exam rather than write a thesis to complete her master's degree requirements is considered to have taken a terminal master's because she is incompletely prepared to produce the kinds of original scholarship the doctorate requires. Similarly, a student required to leave a doctoral program without passing all components such as exams and the dissertation may be awarded a terminal master's in recognition of the fact that they were doing something productive while enrolled.

Two-body problem: Refers to the difficulty of finding two jobs in a single location for two scholars who are part of a couple.

Forming a permanent romantic relationship with another academic entails the possibility that the couple will have to spend at least part of their time living in different locations so that both may hold down jobs in their chosen professions. The problem is partially ameliorated by colleges and universities that engage in "partner hiring."

Sources

....

Voices and Expert Tips in the text that do not have references listed in these source notes come from a qualitative survey conducted with graduate students, from my own experiences and those of graduate students I have known, and from stories related to me informally by former graduate students and their family members.

Chapter 1. So You Want to Go to Graduate School

p. 3, Voice: Pink-lady, re "On choosing between grad school and love," May 14, 2007, http://chronicle.com/forums/.

p. 4, Voice: Prephd, re "Why is grad school so hard?" March 25, 2007, http://chronicle.com/forums/.

p. 5, Voice: Dust Mouse, "How to maintain phocus [*sic*] when bad things are happening to people close to me," June 13, 2007, http://www.phinished.org/.

Chapter 2. Financing Your Education

p. 15, Expert Tip: Dale F. Bloom, Jonathan D. Karp, and Nicholas Cohen, *The Ph.D. Process: A Student's Guide to Graduate School in the Sciences* (New York: Oxford University Press, 1998), 101; emphasis in the original.

p. 17, Voice: Bloom, Karp, and Cohen, *The Ph.D. Process*, 7.

p. 18, Voice: Robert E. Clark and John Palettella, eds., *The Real Guide to Grad School: What You Better Know before You Choose Humanities and Social Sciences* (New York: Lingua Franca Books, 1997), 10.

p. 18, Expert Tip: Jason R. Karp, *How to Survive Your PhD: The Insider's Guide to Avoiding Mistakes, Choosing the Right Program, Working with Professors, and Just How a Person Actually Writes a 200-Page Paper* (Naperville, IL: Sourcebooks, 2009), 6.

p. 19, Voice: Bloom, Karp, and Cohen, *The Ph.D. Process*, 50.

p. 22, Voice: William G. Bowen and Neil L. Rudenstine, *In Pursuit of the PhD* (Princeton, NJ: Princeton University Press, 1992), 286.

Chapter 3. Graduate Expectations

p. 26, Voice: Robert E. Clark and John Palettella, eds., *The Real Guide to Grad School: What You Better Know Before You Choose Humanities and Social Sciences* (New York: Lingua Franca Books, 1997), 18.

p. 27, Voice: Clark and Palettella, *Real Guide to Grad School*, 22.

p. 28, Voice: Krolik, re "Why is grad school so hard?" March 24, 2007, http://chronicle.com/forums/.

p. 30, Voice: Angelica Duran, "One *Mamá's* Dispensible Myths and Indispensible Machines," *Mama PhD: Women Write about Motherhood and Academic Life* (New Brunswick, NJ: Rutgers University Press, 2008), 81.

p. 31, Voice: dundee, re "Wish your family understood," June 26, 2007, http://chronicle.com/forums/.

p. 31, Voice: Clark and Palettella, *Real Guide to Grad School*, 9.

p. 31, Expert Tip: Jason R. Karp, *How to Survive Your PhD: The Insider's Guide to Avoiding Mistakes, Choosing the Right Program, Working with Professors, and Just How a Person Actually Writes a 200-Page Paper* (Naperville, IL: Sourcebooks, 2009), 64.

p. 32, Voice: Steven M. Cahn, *From Student to Scholar: A Candid Guide to Becoming a Professor* (New York: Columbia University Press, 2008), 5.

p. 32, Voice: infopri, re "Wish your family understood," June 29, 2007, http://chronicle.com/forums/.

p. 32, Expert Tip: Gregory M. Colón Semenza, *Graduate Study for the Twenty-First Century: How to Build an Academic Career in the Humanities* (New York: Palgrave Macmillan, 2005), 72.

p. 33, Voice: Cahn, *From Student to Scholar*, 72.

p. 34, Voice: Infopri, re "Why is grad school so hard?" March 25, 2007, http://chronicle.com/forums/.

p. 34, Voice: John A. Goldsmith, John Komlos, and Penny Schine Gold, *The Chicago Guide to Your Academic Career: A Portable Mentor for Scholars from Graduate School through Tenure* (Chicago: University of Chicago Press, 2000), 42–43.

p. 38, Expert Tip: In my tip I quote Jenny K. Hyun, in Hyun et al., "Graduate Student Mental Health: Needs Assessment and Utilization of Counseling Services," *Journal of College Student Development* 47 (2006): 255; and Piper Fogg, in Fogg, "Grad-School Blues," http://chronicle .com, Feb. 20, 2009.

p. 43, Expert Tip: Steven M. Cahn, *Saints and Scamps: Ethics in Academia* (Totowa, NJ: Rowman & Littlefield, 1986),100.

Chapter 4. Coursework is Hard Work

p. 51, Expert Tip: Dale F. Bloom, Jonathan D. Karp, and Nicholas Cohen, *The Ph.D. Process: A Student's Guide to Graduate School in the Sciences* (New York: Oxford University Press, 1998), 43.

p. 51, Voice: Iomhaigh, re "Why is grad school so hard?" March 24, 2007, http://chronicle.com/forums/,

p. 52, Voice: Gregory M. Colón Semenza, *Graduate Study for the Twenty-First Century: How to Build an Academic Career in the Humanities* (New York: Palgrave Macmillan, 2005), 74.

p. 52, Voice: Steven M. Cahn, *Saints and Scamps: Ethics in Academia* (Totowa, NJ: Rowman & Littlefield, 1986), 97.

p. 53, Voice: Bloom, Karp, and Cohen, *The Ph.D. Process*, 105.

p. 58, Voice: Iomhaigh, re "Why is grad school so hard?" March 24, 2007.

p. 60, Expert Tip: Sudhir Venkatesh, *Gang Leader for a Day: A Rogue Sociologist Takes to the Streets* (New York: Penguin Press, 2008), 287–88.

p. 61, Voice: John A. Goldsmith, John Komlos, and Penny Schine Gold, *The Chicago Guide to Your Academic Career: A Portable Mentor for Scholars from Graduate School through Tenure* (Chicago: University of Chicago Press, 2000), 47.

p. 61, Expert Tip: Semenza, *Graduate Study for the Twenty-First Century*, 38.

Chapter 5. Dissertations and Theses

p. 66, Voice: Grasshopper, re "Why is grad school so hard?" March 25, 2007, http://chronicle.com/forums/.

p. 66, Voice: Rosamunde, "I saw a play today! Now questions ab. the Diss and Life!" June 10, 2007, Phinished.org.

p. 70, Expert Tip: Jason R. Karp, *How to Survive Your PhD: The Insider's Guide to Avoiding Mistakes, Choosing the Right Program, Working with Professors, and Just How a Person Actually Writes a 200-Page Paper* (Naperville, IL: Sourcebooks, 2009), 49.

p. 74, Voice: Steven M. Cahn, *Saints and Scamps: Ethics in Academia* (Totowa, NJ: Rowman & Littlefield, 1986), 94–95.

p. 76, Voice: Gradstudent1, re "Why is grad school so hard?" March 24, 2007, http://chronicle.com/forums/.

p. 76, Expert Tip: Gregory M. Colón Semenza, *Graduate Study for the Twenty-First Century: How to Build an Academic Career in the Humanities* (New York: Palgrave Macmillan, 2005), 165.

p. 79, Expert Tip: Dale F. Bloom, Jonathan D. Karp, and Nicholas Cohen, *The Ph.D. Process: A Student's Guide to Graduate School in the Sciences* (New York: Oxford University Press, 1998), 97.

p. 80, Voice: Martha Khan, "The Lady with the Ruler," *BU Today*, Apr. 30, 2009, accessed July 6, 2009, http://www.bu.edu/today/2009/04/29/lady-with-ruler.

Chapter 6. The Academic Culture

p. 84, Voice: John A. Goldsmith, John Komlos, and Penny Schine Gold, *The Chicago Guide to Your Academic Career: A Portable Mentor for Scholars from Graduate School through Tenure* (Chicago: University of Chicago Press, 2000), 261.

p. 85, Voice: Peter J. Feibelman, *A Ph.D. Is Not Enough: A Guide to Survival in Science* (Reading, MA: Addison-Wesley, 1993), 54–55.

Chapter 7. Having a Life in Graduate School

p. 107, Voice: Leonard Cassuto, "Advising the Dissertation Student Who Won't Finish," Oct. 3, 2010, http://chronicle.com.

p. 109, Voice: mad_doctor, re "Ph.D. students & vacation: How long is too long? What do you do?" Dec. 15, 2009, http://chronicle.com/forums/index.php/topic,65119.30.html.

p. 109, Voice: bread_pirate naan, re "Ph.D students & vacation," Dec. 15, 2009, http://chronicle.com/forums.

p. 110, Voice: John A. Goldsmith, John Komlos, and Penny Schine Gold, *The Chicago Guide to Your Academic Career: A Portable Mentor for*

Scholars from Graduate School through Tenure (Chicago: University of Chicago Press, 2000), 39–40.

p. 111, Voice: Goldsmith, Komlos, and Gold, *The Chicago Guide to Your Academic Career*, 249.

p. 113, Expert Tip: Michael T. Nettles and Catherine M. Millett, *Three Magic Letters: Getting to Ph.D.* (Baltimore: Johns Hopkins University Press, 2006), xvii.

p. 113, Voice: Robert Drago, "Harvard and the Academic Glass Ceiling," Mar. 27, 2007, http://chronicle.com/.

p. 114, Voice: Merce, re "Why is grad school so hard?" Mar. 24, 2007, http://chronicle.com/forums/.

Chapter 8. Degrees, Jobs, and Academic Careers

p. 118, Voice: Shamu, re "Why is grad school so hard?" Mar. 24, 2007, http://chronicle.com/forums/.

p. 119, Expert Tip: Jonathan J. Katz, "Full Professor, What's That?" September 7, 2006, http://chronicle.com/.

p. 124, Voice: John A. Goldsmith, John Komlos, and Penny Schine Gold, *The Chicago Guide to Your Academic Career: A Portable Mentor for Scholars from Graduate School through Tenure* (Chicago: University of Chicago Press, 2000), 237.

p. 125, Voice: larryc, re "Dealing with parents while on the job market?" May 9, 2010, http://chronicle.com/forums/.

p. 131, Voice: Goldsmith, Komlos, and Gold, *The Chicago Guide to Your Academic Career*, 240.

p. 132, Voice: carebearstare, re "How hard do you really work?" June 23, 2009, http://chronicle.com/forums/.

Afterword

p. 135, Voice: Edward Nelson, quoted in *Mathematicians: An Outer View of the Inner World*, Mariana Cook, photographer and editor (Princeton: Princeton University Press, 2009), 12.

For Further Reading

....

Basalla, Susan, and Maggie Debelius. *"So What Are You Going to Do with That?" Finding Careers outside Academia*, rev. ed. Chicago: University of Chicago Press, 2007.

A sympathetic and practical advice book for graduate students and graduates who prefer "postacademic" jobs.

Bloom, Dale F., Jonathan D. Karp, and Nicholas Cohen. *The Ph.D. Process: A Student's Guide to Graduate School in the Sciences*. New York: Oxford University Press, 1998.

A straightforward and practical accounting of the particulars of graduate school in the sciences. Some advice applies to nonscientists as well.

Cahn, Steven M. *From Student to Scholar: A Candid Guide to Becoming a Professor*. New York: Columbia University Press, 2008.

In spare and accessible prose, Cahn traces out the professional and social requirements for completing a dissertation and winning tenure as a research professor. Assumes the standard research-based hierarchy of prestige in American universities and that everyone who earns a Ph.D. desires a career as a research professor, with teaching and personal happiness subordinated to that goal.

Clark, Robert E. and John Palattella, eds. *The Real Guide to Grad School: What You Better Know before You Choose Humanities and Social Sciences*. New York: Lingua Franca Books, 1997.

Excellent introduction to the process of graduate study, with field-by-field breakouts of requirements, top schools, and job prospects. Caution: Information about what is hot and who teaches where is dated.

Evans, Elrena, and Caroline Grant, eds. *Mama, PhD: Women Write about Motherhood and Academic Life.* New Brunswick, NJ: Rutgers University Press, 2008.

Literary essays about work-life balance issues for women in the academy. Required reading for anyone considering having children as a graduate student or professor.

Feibelman, Peter J. *A Ph.D. Is Not Enough: A Guide to Survival in Science.* Reading, MA: Addison-Wesley, 1993.

This wise little book explains what it means to have a scientific career, whether inside or outside the academy. It emphasizes practical behavioral skills that scientists can add to their repertoire to showcase their research in a light that will communicate the long-term potential of the scholar's contributions. Although it is older than other advice manuals, it is not dated.

Frank, Fredrick and Karl Stein. *Playing the Game: The Streetsmart Guide to Graduate School,* "new and/or improved edition." New York: iUniverse, 2004.

A practical guide to the culture, students, and faculty of graduate school. Encourages being a smart-alec and "playing the game" with attitude. Caution: Assumes that all dissertations follow the social science model that the authors were required to use in writing their theses.

Goldsmith, John A., John Komlos, and Penny Schine Gold, *The Chicago Guide to Your Academic Career: A Portable Mentor for Scholars from Graduate School through Tenure.* Chicago: University of Chicago Press, 2000.

Thoughtful commentary on graduate school and the early years of a professor's career. Written as a conversation among the three authors and an anonymous interlocutor. Notably, the authors feel free to disagree with one another on certain points.

Gray, Paul, and David E. Drew. *What They Didn't Teach You in Graduate School: 199 Helpful Hints for Success in Your Academic Career.* Sterling, VA: Stylus, 2008.

A compilation of advice for graduate students and early career professors. Some hints are truly insightful; others make the mistake of assuming that the advice from the authors' disciplines applies generally.

Jellison, Jerald M. *Life after Grad School: Getting from A to B*. Oxford: Oxford University Press, 2010.

Guidance for academics looking to move from a university setting to the business world. Most of the advice is generically applicable for those seeking professional positions, but the book includes some useful insights about how the strengths that lead one into graduate school can be translated into terms appealing to nonacademic employers.

Karp, Jason R. *How to Survive Your PhD: An Insider's Guide to Avoiding Mistakes, Choosing the Right Program, Working with Professors, and Just How a Person Actually Writes a 200-Page Paper*. Naperville, IL: Sourcebooks, 2009.

Suggestions for not replicating the doctoral career of the author, who failed his preliminary exam and completed his dissertation at a different university from the one where he earned his degree in exercise physiology. Makes generalizations based on his personal and disciplinary experiences. A better fit for students in the sciences than in the humanities.

Peters, Robert L. *Getting What You Came For: The Smart Student's Guide to Earning a Master's or Ph.D.*, rev. ed. New York: Noonday Press, 1997.

Detailed explanation relevant to all the steps of graduate school, from applying to finding an academic job.

Rittner, Barbara, and Patricia Trudeau. *The Women's Guide to Surviving Graduate School*. Thousand Oaks, CA: Sage, 1997.

Practical advice for women on considering, applying to, and attending graduate school.

Ruben, Adam. *Surviving Your Stupid, Stupid Decision to Go to Grad School*. New York: Broadway Books, 2010.

Primarily a sarcastic commentary on the miseries of graduate school, written for people who already know what graduate school is like. The only moderately serious advice appears in the epilogue.

Rugg, Gordon, and Marian Petre. *The Unwritten Rules of PhD Research*. Maindenhead, England: Open University Press, 2004.

Useful ideas for getting through graduate school, including discussions of such unexplained mysteries as a literature review. Caution: Written expressly for British academics, this book contains culturally specific terminology and assumes familiarity with the British university system.

Semenza, Gregory M. Colón. *Graduate Study for the Twenty-first Century: How to Build an Academic Career in the Humanities*. New York: Palgrave Macmillan, 2005.

Begins with the premise that any graduate student in the humanities who aspires to an academic career should behave like a professional from day one. This book is thus a guide to acting like an assistant professor from the start of graduate school, with a consistent emphasis on overpreparation. This advice is sound, given the state of the tenure-track job market, but makes the prospect of graduate study even more intimidating than it already is.

Toth, Emily. *Ms. Mentor's Impeccable Advice for Women in Academia*. Philadelphia: University of Pennsylvania Press, 1997; also *Ms. Mentor's New and Ever More Impeccable Advice for Women and Men in Academia*. Philadelphia: University of Pennsylvania Press, 2009.

Compilations of Ms. Mentor's irreverent and witty advice column from the *Chronicle of Higher Education* about how to get along in the academy. Not only for women.

Index

vacation. *See* time off

women, 41, 74, 87, 113–115,
125–126, 154, 155, 156
writing, 46–47, 63, 132, 133; sample
of, for job applications, 120, 121;
strategy for, 54–55, 77–78; time
involved in, 28, 43, 74–75